Angry Teens and the Parents Who Love Them

Sandy J. Austin

Beacon Hill Press of Kansas City
Kansas City, Missouri

Copyright 2002
by Beacon Hill Press of Kansas City

ISBN 083-411-982X

Printed in the
United States of America

Cover Design: Kevin Williamson

Library of Congress Cataloging-in-Publication Data

Austin, Sandy.
    Angry teens and the parents who love them / Sandy Austin.
        p. cm.
Includes bibliographical references.
    ISBN 0-8341-1982-X (Paperback)
    1. Parenting—Religious aspects—Christianity. 2. Parent and teenager—Religious aspects—Christianity. 3. Christian teenagers—Religious life. 4. Anger—Religious aspects—Christianity.
I. Title.
    BV2529 .A97 2002
    248.8'45—dc21   2002005754

10   9   8   7   6   5   4   3   2   1

For my mom, Dora Austin,
who believed in me and inspired me to dream my dreams!
Mom, when God handpicked you to be my mother,
He chose the best in all the world!
I love you!

Contents

Youth rage and murder are escalating at a shocking rate, leading to more shootings, bombings, and killings by young people in school hallways and on quiet suburban streets. . . . What causes our teenagers to lash out at their parents, teachers, and peers with such lethal violence? What has happened in our culture to allow mere children to become so callous and violent?"

—from Josh McDowell's *The Disconnected Generation*

Foreword

In April 1999 we were stunned as we watched Columbine High School students fleeing from their school in terror, trying to escape the murderous rampage two of their fellow students were carrying out inside. But the tragedy at Columbine is only one blatant example of a pervasive problem we are seeing at all levels of society. Anger in today's youth culture is careening out of control. From withdrawal to rebellion, from drugs to school shootings, parents are seeing their children's anger rising and being manifested in new and disturbing ways. And all around the country adults are left searching for answers as to how they can help their children.

I witnessed the devastating aftermath of the Columbine shootings firsthand when I visited Littleton, Colorado, shortly after that horrific day. Among other activities, I led a training session for youth workers and counselors working with students and parents affected by the tragedy. That's where I met Sandy Austin.

As a school counselor helping those impacted by the tragedy and in her various roles over the last 25 years, Sandy has helped thousands of young people struggling with anger problems. She has also worked with many children who have been on the receiving end of someone else's anger. In that time Sandy has seen what works and what doesn't. And through her experiences, she has gained valuable insight for parents dealing with angry kids of their own.

In the pages that follow, Sandy shares practical advice on topics such as unearthing the roots and reasons behind your child's anger, avoiding common pitfalls on the path to raising a healthy teenager, and finding effective ways to address an angry teen. In doing so, she offers something more to parents and others who have a heart to help their hurting teens—she offers glimmers of hope.

—Josh D. McDowell

Acknowledgments

I would like to express my appreciation to the staff of Beacon Hill Press of Kansas City—especially Bonnie Perry and Jeanette Gardner Littleton—for having the courage to address the hurt and pain of parents of angry kids. Lives will be touched as a result of your vision.

I am so thankful to my mom, Dora Austin, who has believed in me and has spent many late nights looking over the manuscript and laboring from afar while I was up late working on the book. Miles Austin, my brother, how can I thank you for the laptop to help make the writing process more feasible? I also want to thank my other two siblings, Cheryl Hull and Paul Austin, for their support and encouragement throughout the process.

I also thank the following people who assisted me in the editing and preparation of the manuscript: Marlene Bagnull, Marlene Depler, and Debbie Ward; and my writing mentors: Marlene Bagnull, Judy Couchman, and Virelle Kidder.

Thanks also to Denise Ulmer and BrookLynn Rose for so freely sharing their pain so others can be "comforted with the comfort they have received" and to the other people whose stories have been shared in this book. Thank you for your courage to live.

I would be remiss to forget the many prayer warriors who carried me through writer's block and exhaustion. I pray that God will richly bless you.

Introduction

I deal with angry teens every day. In fact, just 24 hours before I was approached about writing this book, I spent the entire day dealing with two very angry students. As a school counselor I have had a front-row seat for the escalating epidemic of adolescent anger.

I have seen the look of confusion on parents' faces as they struggle to understand the root of their teen's anger. I've heard committed, caring parents brand themselves as failures as their child is suspended from school as a result of anger-related issues. I have counseled adults who fear their own mistakes as parents have marked their children for life. And I have listened and sympathized as parents have cried out in desperation, "I don't know how to reach my child anymore!"

If you fall into one or more of these categories, either as a parent, concerned relative, friend, or youth worker, you will find hope in the pages that follow. I will share valuable tools that will help you through the maze of anger issues in your adolescent. Not every tool works with every teen, and if at any time you fear for your own safety or the safety of your teen or anyone else, seek professional help immediately from your local church, community, or law enforcement agency. Even if your child is not willing to accept help, you must seek the support you need.

I wish I could talk with you personally to encourage you with the victories of other parents who have made it through tumultuous times—and I'll share some of those stories with you in this book. Take courage. There is light at the end of the tunnel. Press on!

1

Anger Unleashed

Screaming sirens. Hovering helicopters. Flashing lights. Yellow crime tape. No amount of training could have prepared me for what I was about to face.

Students streamed out of Columbine High School in Littleton, Colorado, with their hands on their heads like criminals. Mothers cradled shell-shocked daughters. Fathers frantically ran to embrace their sons. The scenes on television mesmerized us. Our assistant principal broke my fixed gaze. "All school district counselors need to report to Columbine immediately. Go!"

I ran to my car, turned on the radio, and headed toward Columbine. Screeching tires pierced the tension as I swerved to miss a car that cut me off. People drove recklessly with their attention focused on the radio updates instead of the road. The typically 20-minute drive took a heart-pounding 40 minutes.

As I turned onto the main road leading to Columbine, I prayed in desperation. *Lord, what do I say to these people? I don't want to say the wrong thing. Please give me the right words for each person.*

Columbine High School was completely blocked off, so I was detoured to nearby Leawood Elementary. The streets were crammed with four times the number of vehicles they were designed to hold. An abandoned car with its door open and signal light still flashing blocked a lane. Streams of people heading toward Leawood darted between cars. Media vans jumped the curbs to park on the grass. Police from every jurisdiction swarmed the area on ground and in the air. The closest parking spot was three blocks away. Once I parked, the magnitude of the situation penetrated deeper

11

with each step I took toward Leawood. *Lord, give me wisdom for each situation. Help me to calm down, Lord. Please help me.*

I arrived at 1:00 P.M. and squeezed my way through the hordes of onlookers and media. Flashing my I.D., I pushed through the main doors into the chaos inside and into the gym.

Lines of parents, reunited and clinging to their kids feverishly, signed their names as they attempted to escape the pandemonium. Students sobbed and hugged each other. Parents paced, their eyes darting through the gym, searching for their sons and daughters. Instructions announced from the front of the gym were drowned out by the shrill ringing of cell phones. Anxiety contorted faces. Fear crawled the walls.

Buses began arriving with the precious cargo from Columbine. The Columbine students entering the gym were corralled to the gym's stage. As parents saw their frightened teenagers come in, screams of relief raised to the rafters. Yet for other parents the wait continued.

I began to mingle to see how I could help, still asking, *God, lead me to the people You want to reach through me.* A couple near the back of the gym caught my attention. They showed a calm beneath the fear. The woman's wind-blown brown hair revealed that she had been unexpectedly snatched from her daily routine. The man, dressed in business attire, must have rushed from his job. Who were they waiting for—a son or daughter? What thoughts were running through their minds?

I eased over to them, introduced myself, and asked whom they were waiting for. "Our son," the woman said. I asked his name. "Justin Thompson,* and our names are Kim and Dave," she replied.

"What grade is Justin in?" I asked.

"He's a 10th grader," Kim replied.

I sensed that they didn't want to talk anymore, so I didn't

---

*All names are fictitious.

press any further. "I'll be listening for Justin's name, too, and if it's all right, I'll check in with you every once in a while to see if you've heard anything."

"Thanks, Sandy. We appreciate your help."

They personified the hope mixed with fear that filled the room. I prayed as I walked to another area of the gym. *Lord, be with Justin wherever he is, and be with Kim and Dave too.*

I talked with other parents and students. The lists of names from the incoming buses rang out from the police chief's bullhorn. Students came off the buses either crying or whooping and hollering. At times when I missed hearing the names, I looked across the gym to the Thompsons. They shook their heads, letting me know Justin had not been found yet.

The hours dragged on, fewer buses came, and the gym atmosphere became even more solemn. Tables overflowed with donated food and drinks, but as the hours passed, everyone's appetite diminished. I checked in with the Thompsons periodically to see if they had heard Justin's name.

At about 6:30 P.M. a question rang from the back of the gym, "Are any more buses coming?" A deafening silence fell on the crowd.

The answer pierced the stillness: "No." I looked over at the Thompsons, and their heads dropped.

The police officials and coroner announced that it would still be hours before they could get final word on each missing student. They asked for detailed information from the parents about their kids, including dental records, for identification purposes. Gasps rang out, and reality hit. The officials assured the parents that their sons and daughters could still be hiding in the school, but they also acknowledged fatalities.

Some time later, one woman's daughter, who must have just come from a dental office, handed her mother a blue cardboard box. The mother opened the box and took out the plaster impressions of her son's teeth. She grasped them in her hands for a few moments, as if she were longing for any connection with her missing son. The sight pierced my heart.

Soon the Thompsons and about 16 other families sat in circles of chairs surrounded by their friends and family. After waiting for hours, the Thompsons went home, hoping to be awakened in the middle of the night with news that Justin was found hiding in the school.

Of the eight families I worked with most closely that day, six families saw sons or daughters enter the gym—but two didn't. At 9:30 P.M., I left Leawood, exhausted.

The heaviness in the air remained over the next few days as I spent long hours counseling students and parents. I was so busy counseling that I didn't get to see any newspapers or news programs, so I didn't know if Justin had been found dead or alive.

But Kim Thompson kept coming to my mind. Her increasing anguish on the day of the shootings was etched in my thoughts. I prayed for her every day. On the weekend, I picked up the newspaper and saw a picture of Kim and Dave at Justin's funeral. Tears streamed down my face. The picture haunted me.

In the past, I had frequently worked with parents of teenagers with anger issues, but this was the first time I had worked with parents who had experienced such an enormous loss at the hands of angry teens. The magnitude of it deeply affected me for months. As a counselor, I had learned to hold back my own feelings so I could effectively counsel others, but this task was monumental.

Six months later I saw Kim at a special luncheon during a women's conference. I had known she would be there, so I prepared myself to be available if she needed me.

Kim was surrounded by a group of women. I was glad she had established a support network, but suddenly a flood of emotions hit me. For six months I had been strong for everyone else. I had not processed my own grief. I had not realized how much the tragedy had affected me. Now the tears flowed, bringing healing.

The tragedy at Columbine High School still affects thousands of people today. When the gunmen unleashed their pent-up anger on their school on April 20, 1999, 12 students and one teacher were dead four hours later, plus the shooters. More than 25 students and staff were critically wounded, and many others also have scars that run straight through their hearts.

My experience with the kids, parents, and staff at Columbine High School has touched me deeply. They inspire me with the courage they showed the world. The students and parents from Columbine have survived, with many scars and residual effects, one of the most horrific incidents imaginable.

School shootings are an uncommon manifestation of unresolved anger. Anger has escalated among youth in the last decade and is reaching epidemic proportions. Society is impacted more than ever by the prevalence and severity of such problems. Not until we understand the magnitude of the problem will we be able to turn the situation around.

> Parent Power Point: **As we understand the severity and magnitude of anger in our society, we'll be able to help our teens deal with anger in their own lives.**

The ripple effect of anger can be devastating. But there's hope. After difficulties strike, we can pick up the pieces of our lives through the healing process. Like a wound that changes to a scar on our skin, eventually the searing pain subsides, though we see visible reminders. Some are able to take the lessons from their own scars and ease the pain of others.

What Is Anger?

The incident at Columbine may seem like an extreme example of anger. It is drastic, but it also shows us what anger can grow to if unchecked or ignored.

Anger is a natural part of life. We all deal with it. The Bible acknowledges anger: "'In your anger do not sin': Do not let the sun go down while you are still angry" (Eph. 4:26). Even Jesus got angry in the Temple in Jerusalem. God gave us the emotion of anger to help us detect when something's wrong. When our teens have anger in their lives, it's an indication that something's wrong, that there's some issue they need to deal with.

The key is how we deal with our anger. Some people blow up, destroying those around them. Others ignore their anger until it seeps out through inappropriate coping mechanisms, or they hold it in until it explodes in one great burst. These responses are unhealthy and hurt everyone involved.

Some people, when confronted with their anger, will want help getting it under control. Education about anger and some form of accountability might take care of the situation. Others may need to have an intervention meeting with family members to confront that person regarding what his or her anger is costing all those involved. At other times the anger may be effectively treated through a pastoral or professional counselor and a formal counseling process.

In my high school counseling office, I work almost daily with young people and parents dealing with the results of anger in their lives. In this book I'll share with you stories of kids and parents I've worked with who were on a path headed toward destruction but turned their lives around. The names and some identifying characteristics have been changed to protect their privacy.

> Parent Power Point: If your teen is dealing with anger, know that you're not alone. Other parents are there, and other parents have been through this.

In one book we cannot possibly address all the various aspects of anger, so the focus of *Angry Teens and the Parents Who Love Them* will be a more practical discussion of anger instead of a theoretical, clinical approach to the subject. We will discuss the many faces of anger, why young people struggle with anger more now than ever before, how to prevent anger from getting out of control, how to address your child's anger, and parent survival tools as you confront your child's anger.

Questions

Many parents of teenagers are at their wit's end in dealing with their son's or daughter's anger. Anguished parents have often called me in desperation. Their child was having problems in school or at home with not doing chores, lying, stealing, being truant, using drugs or alcohol, practicing promiscuous or risk-taking behavior, being in trouble with the law, or any number of other problems. They had tried everything they knew to reach their kids but to no avail.

These parents are asking:

My daughter seems angry at the world. How can I reach her?

My son is beginning risky behaviors. What should I do?

Could my child ever be a victim of a school shooting?

How can I really know my daughter?

What does it take for an adolescent to reach the point of violence?

What behaviors signal a red flag regarding my son or daughter?

How can I communicate with my adolescents to find out how they're really doing?

Are you a parent who's asking similar questions? Do you have a young person out of control? Do you have a son or daughter beginning to show signs of anger or beginning to run with the wrong crowd? Is your kid depressed? You're not alone.

> **Parent Power Point: If adolescents have a significant adult who believes in them and is willing to invest in their lives, they have an increased chance of a bright future.**

You may be a grandparent or relative concerned about a young person. Or you may be a professional looking for resources. I believe this book will give you some tools to help you recognize anger-related problems and know how to address them. If adolescents have a significant adult who believes in them and is willing to invest in their lives, they have an increased chance of a bright future.

Where Does God Fit into All This?

God knows what you're going through. He sees how you've struggled to help your son or daughter. He knows your children better than you do, because He created them— He specifically gave them unique personalities. He's just as vested in this process as you are, because He has great plans for your kids. "'For I know the plans I have for you,' declares the LORD, 'plans to prosper you and not to harm you, plans to give you hope and a future'" (Jer. 29:11). That verse can give you hope as a parent and for your children. But make sure you don't stop there. The next couple of verses hold a key to getting through this process. "Then you will call upon me and come and pray to me, and I will listen to you. You will seek me and find me when you seek me with all your heart" (Jer. 29:12-13).

S. D. Gordon said, "You can do more than pray after you have prayed, but you cannot do more than pray till you have prayed."[1] Prayer is the key to addressing your child's anger whether it is as violent as a school shooting or as simple as slamming a door. At times you may feel like throwing in the towel and giving up on this whole parenting thing. Or you may lay your head on the pillow at night with tears in your eyes while feeling like a failure as a parent. You think, *How can my child turn out this way if I'm not a horrible parent?* You beat yourself up trying to figure out where you went wrong. God understands.

Parent Power Point: Prayer is the key to addressing your child's anger—whether it is as violent as a school shooting or as simple as slamming a door.

He speaks to you—

"Come to me, all you who are weary and burdened, and I will give you rest. Take my yoke upon you and learn from me, for I am gentle and humble in heart, and you will find rest for your souls. For my yoke is easy and my burden is light. . . . My thoughts are not your thoughts, neither are your ways my ways. . . . As the heavens are higher than the earth, so are my ways higher than your ways and my thoughts than your thoughts." . . . If any of you lacks wisdom, he should ask God, who gives generously to all without finding fault, and it will be given to him" *(Matt. 11:28-30; Isa. 55:8-9; James 1:5)*.

You may remember the poem "Footprints" that was especially popular in the 1980s. It tells of a person walking through life on the beach with God, and as he looked back he noticed that during the toughest times there was only one set of footprints. The man accused God of abandoning him during those times, but God corrected him, saying that it was during those times that God carried him. Deut. 33:12 depicts us as snuggled in God's arms: "Let the beloved of the LORD rest secure in him, for he shields him all day long, and the one the LORD loves rests between his shoulders." Let God carry you through this process of dealing with your child's anger.

Parent Power Point: Let God carry you through this process of dealing with your child's anger.

God will take care of you and your son or daughter. He will give you the resources you need—through the Bible, this book, your church, people He will bring into your life, and so on. Ask Him, and He will lead you each step of the way. Right now it may seem impossible to find a resolution to your situation. You may feel like Paul in 2 Cor. 4:8-9: "We are hard pressed on every side, but not crushed; perplexed, but not in despair; persecuted, but not abandoned; struck down, but not destroyed." Hopefully Jesus' words in John 16:33 are reassuring to you: "I have told you these things, so that in me you will have peace. In this world you will have trouble. But take heart! I have overcome the world."

If God created all of us and the universe, He should know the best way to handle your child. Ask Him for help. He longs to help you and strengthen you for the journey ahead. His promise in Isa. 40:28-31 should give you courage to press on: "Do you not know? Have you not heard? The LORD is the everlasting God, the Creator of the ends of the earth. He will not grow tired or weary, and his understanding no one can fathom. He gives strength to the weary and increases the power of the weak. Even youths grow tired and weary, and young men stumble and fall; but those who hope in the LORD will renew their strength. They will soar on wings like eagles; they will run and not grow weary, they will walk and not be faint." That's the hope that can carry us through this process.

It will take courage to delve into the problem of your child's anger, but it will be worth it in the end. What you have seen in your child may just be the tip of the iceberg. The first step we must take is acknowledging our children's anger and realizing the degree to which it affects all of our lives.

Action Steps

1. What prompted you to pick up this book?
2. When you finish the last page of this book, what do you hope you will have learned?
3. How has your child's anger affected your life?
4. How would you like it to change?
5. You may feel weary of the struggle with your child's anger issues, yet there's still hope. You may feel emotionally battered and bruised, but God's promise for you is in 2 Cor. 4:8-9: "We are hard pressed on every side, but not crushed; perplexed, but not in despair; persecuted, but not abandoned; struck down, but not destroyed." He will sustain you through this process. Write out a prayer from your heart stating that you desire God's help in dealing with your child's anger and that you need His help and strength to see you through the process.

2
The Faces of Anger

John's dad, Dave, called me at school to talk about his son's drinking problem. John had been suspended from school for five days for having a couple of drinks at his friend's house after school and then coming to a concert at school. An administrator had smelled the alcohol.

Exasperated, Dave said, "Sandy, this is the third time since the beginning of school that John has been caught drinking." He was a popular 9th grader at school. He and his friends had started hanging around some 11th graders who had a reputation for drinking. "I thought we brought up John right. We don't have alcohol in our house, and we've taught John the dangers of it. I don't know what to do. Where have we gone wrong?"

I talked with John after his suspension. I learned that at the beginning of the school year, his father had made stricter rules for John, knowing the freedom in high school could leave too much temptation for John. John started drinking because he knew it would infuriate his dad.

Parent Power Point: Anger in teens' lives is not surprising, considering all the pressures most teens face today.

Times Have Changed

Today's teens face tremendous pressures more than ever before. In 1940 teachers rated the top disciplinary problems in schools:
Talking out of turn

Chewing gum
Making noise
Running in the halls
Cutting in line
Dress code violations

The teachers of today have rated the following as the top disciplinary problems in schools:

Drug abuse
Alcohol abuse
Pregnancy
Suicide
Rape
Robbery and assault[1]

Anger has been around since the beginning of time, but it has escalated to a point that our daily lives are impacted by the resulting behaviors.

Parent Power Point: Teen anger usually falls into one of two categories: public anger and masked anger.

Adolescent anger can be split into two categories: public anger and masked anger. Typically students have a tendency toward one form or the other. Public anger harms another person and is often witnessed in the home, community, schools, and so on. Masked anger is often lived out in isolation, usually impacting others indirectly. This type of anger is masked because it is typically manifested by at-risk behavior with the intention of harming self.

I believe masked anger is just as widespread as public anger among young people. I have worked in public schools as well as Christian schools. I have also worked with young people in a full-time ministry. The schools I've worked in have ranged from elementary through high school, from rural to urban, from affluent to poor, and from an enrollment of 150 to almost 2,000. In working with thousands of kids, I've found that persons typically stereotype angry kids as tough, at-risk, disadvantaged, disrespectful, wearing baggy pants, sporting a baseball cap on backwards, smoking a cigarette, using filthy language, and so on. But I've found the same type of anger in every school or ministry I've worked in—often when the kids don't show any of these characteristics.

I found that masked anger was more prevalent in the Christian, rural, and affluent schools than the public, poor, and urban schools. Thus, the general public perception is that anger issues are worse in the latter schools. Perhaps this is why many people have been shocked by the school shootings, saying, "I never thought anything like this could happen in our school," or "I left my other school because of the threats of violence. I heard this was one of the safest schools in the area."

Anger was present—it was just masked. And masked anger can eventually erupt into public anger, as it did at Columbine. Yet all around us in society and in the news, the greatest media coverage we see concerns public anger.

Public Anger

One manifestation of anger that has recently received the most media attention is school violence, which has escalated dramatically in the last few years. From February 2, 1996, to March 7, 2001, 15 incidents of school violence resulted in many injuries and 36 deaths. During that time the media reported 11 similar plans thwarted by law enforcement officials. And countless other incidents go unnoticed by the television cameras. According to a Gallup poll, 20 percent of students 13 to 17 years of age said their schools had been evacuated because of bomb threats.[2]

We probably all remember threats from a bully in our school days. Bullying has been around as long as schools have existed and has been a key factor in school violence. Yet many of today's bullies use more violent threats of harm to their victims and have the means to carry out those threats. The severity of the threat directly correlates to the degree of unresolved anger. Ten percent of students who drop out of school do so from fear of bullying. Also, 162,000 students stay home each day to avoid being bullied, and 20 percent of high school students are afraid to go into rest rooms at school because of bullying.[3]

Fighting is also more rampant today, with 20 percent of teens reporting that they were in a fight sometime in the previous year.[4]

I have seen a rise in all types of abuse as society has become more violent. Domestic violence is an ever-present concern as our society's pace and stress levels increase each year. Forty percent of teenage girls 14-17 report knowing someone their age who has been hit or beaten by a boyfriend. Also, 50 percent of men who frequently assault their wives also abuse their children.[5]

> Parent Power Point: In an angry society, sometimes our teens date people who have problems with anger. If you have any reason to suspect a boyfriend or girlfriend might be abusing your teen, don't ignore your instincts—look into the situation.

"Ms. Austin, Tiffany's mom beat her up last night—she has bruises on her face and body," Jenna said with tears in her eyes. Four months earlier, I had made a social services report for a similar incident with Tiffany's mother.

I went to Tiffany's classroom and was stunned by the two-inch bruise under her eye. Tiffany told me her mother had dragged her by the hair into her bedroom, threw her on the bed, sat on her, and pounded her face and body. She had five big bruises on her body. As she left for school that morning, her mother had said, "I'll be by later to withdraw you from school so you won't have the chance to tell them what happened." Tiffany told me that her mother was mad at her live-in boyfriend but took that anger out on Tiffany.

Later that morning, Tiffany's mother stormed into the school. Her face was red, her eyes bulged, and the veins on her neck looked ready to burst. She was a big woman, and frankly,

I was scared of her. I can imagine Tiffany's fear. Charges were brought, but a settlement was reached out of court.

Anger can be related to sexual abuse and assault as perpetrators use it to gain power over the other person. One in every three women will be sexually assaulted some time in her life. Date rape is also becoming more prevalent.

As I face these types of situations daily, I've found that only by God's grace, strength, and wisdom can I keep a positive attitude. I believe we can reach these kids, kids like those whose stories I share. Even though many of the struggles of the students I deal with tear at my heart, I would rather be in the middle of them than on the sidelines. We must all courageously face these issues. Our society has ignored them for too long.

Another face of anger exists in a much more obscure and subtle form. These are the kids who mask their anger.

Masked Anger

Teens can easily hide the symptoms of anger from the adults in their lives. Probably the most prevalent type of masked anger is depression. Depression has been described as anger turned inward. Often the result of difficult situations out of a person's control, a sense of helplessness or powerlessness can lead to depression.

> Parent Power Point: **Your teen may not even realize that anger is a natural emotion. You can help your teen by letting him or her express anger in appropriate ways.**
>
> **For instance, if your daughter seems angry, take the step to ask, "You seem upset. Is something wrong? Are you angry about something?"**
>
> **Giving your teen a chance to talk and responding in a nonjudgmental way will show that you care and will also help your teen calm down and approach anger constructively.**

Also, depression often develops in people who have learned to suppress their feelings. Many have learned either that it's not safe to express their emotions or that being angry is bad. If we don't learn that anger is a natural emotion (as some would say, "Being angry is OK; being mean is not"), we will be afraid or embarrassed to show it. It may appear that the only other option is to hide it. Some may be afraid to release their anger because they don't know if they'll be able to control it. A former student of mine was afraid to show her anger because she had learned that anger is bad.

Nicole moved to our school from another state where she had been a cheerleader, a student government leader, an honors student, and a popular classmate. She came to our school in the middle of the year because of her father's job transfer.

Nicole couldn't get involved in cheerleading or student government at our school since they were already in progress. Some of the popular girls in school were jealous of Nicole's great personality and beauty, so they ostracized her. Since she believed being angry was bad, she didn't share her hurt and frustration with anyone. She thought she had to "keep a stiff upper lip." Every day after school, she spent hours in her bedroom studying or listening to music. She began to eat junk food out of boredom.

Her mom, Judy, called me, saying, "I'm concerned about Nicole. She seems lonely. She hides out in her room all evening and is gaining weight from eating so much junk food. She's a different person. I think she's depressed."

In talking to Judy, I found out that Nicole had been very involved in a church youth group where they used to live, but they hadn't found a new church home yet. Judy said they would try a church with an active youth group—that could be a place where Nicole could get plugged in to make some new friends.

At first it was difficult for Nicole to meet other youth group members. She had lost her confidence. Some of the girls reached out to her and included her in their group of friends. As she participated in the activities, she felt more at home and began to regain her confidence. She was asked to join the worship team. Instead of spending lonely evenings in her bedroom, she began hanging out with her new friends. Gradually she came out of her depression, stopped eating poorly, and lost the weight she had gained from the junk food.

Several months later, she joined the youth group's leadership team. She began to thrive. When a new girl came into the youth group, Nicole reached out to her. Nicole asked the youth director if she could start an outreach ministry to help new teens in the youth group fit in more quickly. She found purpose again, and her depression and internal anger subsided. She used her pain to meet others' needs.

> **Indications That Your Teen May Be Dealing with Masked Anger:**
> **Uncharacteristic isolation**
> **Depression**
> **Eating disorders**
> **Self-mutilation**
> **Acting out with behavior such as drinking or doing drugs**

Other Faces of Anger

Eating disorders can result from masked anger. A female who diets before the age of 14 is eight times more likely to develop an eating disorder, and 52 percent of adolescent females report dieting before the age of 14.[6] Kids with eating disorders embody an anger taken out on themselves. Some girls with eating disorders may also have cuts on their arms from self-mutilation. In 1988, 750 per 100,000 of the population exhibited self-injurious behavior, but more recent estimates are that 1,000 per 100,000, or 1 percent, self-injure.[7]

One self-cutter's anger became public anger. Just minutes after attending a mass honoring the Santee High School shooting victims in California, she walked into her school cafeteria and shot a classmate in the shoulder. She then placed the gun against her own temple. School staff and another student talked her out of pulling the trigger. The girl had been bullied at school and had even been pelted with stones once at a previous school. She had become depressed, started skipping classes, and even resorted to self-mutilation.[8]

Alcohol and drug abuse are other at-risk behaviors that may indicate anger issues. I have heard kids say they have used drugs to escape their frustrations with situations out of their control. When they were high, they didn't feel their anger any more. Alcohol use is the No. 1 drug problem among young people.[9] Kids who drink alcohol are 7.5 times more likely to use an illicit drug, and 50 times more likely to use cocaine, than those who never drink alcohol.[10]

Another form of masked anger for parents to note is the normal anger that seems to come as our teens assert their independence. In their high school years, young people exhibit quiet rumblings and subversive methods such as sneaking out at night, staying out past curfew, and so on to seek more freedom. While that yearning and longing for independence is normal, it is still frustrating to parents.

A friend of mine Marlene told me about the process she endured with one of her daughters. Each year in high school, Marlene gave her daughter more and more freedom, but the daughter was never satisfied—she kept pushing the envelope. Finally Marlene talked to her about it.

"Honey, each year I keep giving you a little more freedom, but you keep resisting boundary lines. It's as if the fence around your pasture expands each year, but you're always pushing against the gate. You're never satisfied. Eventually I'll fling that gate open and let you run free, but until then I need to keep that fence around you and the gate closed. Even though it may be hard, try to trust me."

Her daughter finally agreed that her mom's observations were accurate. Her rebellious tendencies lessened, and their relationship improved.

Teens often express anger as they resist boundaries and

struggle for independence. As parents, we must steady ourselves and hold to an appropriate course until it's time to let go. In her daughter's graduation card, Marlene wrote, "I've opened the gate! Run free! The world's your pasture!"

> **Parent Power Point: As parents, we must steady ourselves and hold to an appropriate course until it's time to let go.**

Fear can also be expressed in the form of anger. Marlene also said that as the time approached for her other daughter to leave for college, the two of them began arguing over small matters. Fear of the unknown and leaving home were the basis for this daughter's anger. Anger may be about fear in the parents as they release their children into the world and grieve the loss of the relationship as they have known it. The parents know their relationship with that son or daughter will never be the same again. It's as if the rise in anger, frustration, and frequent arguments give us the energy and momentum to part and say our good-byes. It's easier to let someone go when we're mad.

> **Parent Power Point: Angry behavior may indicate that your teen has some fears about the future or about other aspects of life that he feels are out of his control.**

As we have seen in this chapter, anger may be very easy or extremely difficult to spot in our children. An awareness of public anger versus masked anger will help us know which type our kids may be dealing with.

The statistics about anger in our society can be overwhelming and even discouraging; however, we need to be aware of the magnitude of the issues our young people confront. We must know what we're facing in order to be able to effectively help our teens.

Action Steps

1. Does your child struggle more with public anger or masked anger?
2. In what ways does your child act out the anger?
3. How have you tried to deal with the anger?
4. What has not worked in addressing the anger?
5. If you're not sure about the extent of the anger, look at the "fruit" of your teen's life. In Matt. 7:20 we read these words of Jesus: "By their fruit you will recognize them." Write a prayer for discernment to see all the ways your child manifests anger.

3

The Reasons Our Kids Are Angry

"Mrs. Bernardo told me I needed to see you," Tabitha said as she walked into my office.

"What's up—need help with your geophysics?" I joked since Tabitha knew I never got that far in high school science. By her drooping shoulders, I could tell something was wrong.

Hesitantly sitting, she continued, "My mom hit me last night, but it wasn't my fault."

"What happened?" I asked. I had already heard that Tabitha had cheated on a test in another class the week before, and the day before, she had been caught changing her grade in Mrs. Bernardo's grade book.

Tabitha continued: "My mom started yelling at me about changing my grade in Mrs. Bernardo's grade book; then I yelled back." She pulled her hair away from the right side of her face and revealed a bruise the size of a half-dollar. "Then she pushed me into the cabinet door. I ran to my bedroom and locked the door."

Whenever school officials see a bruise on students resulting from another person or themselves, we are legally required to report it to the authorities, which I did. When Tabitha's mom came to the school, she stormed into my office, hovered over Tabitha, and raged, saying, "You've not only messed up your own life, but now you're messing up my life and these people's lives as well. Are you proud of yourself?"

Tabitha shot back, "Well, you don't care about me. You don't know me. All you want me to be is 'Little Miss Prissy.'

31

Well, I'm *not* 'Little Miss Prissy.' I'm pretty neat—if you would just take the time to get to know me!" Tears gushed from her eyes.

As we checked into the situation, we found that Tabitha had been lying to her mom for months. She had moved into her mom's home after several years of living with her dad, an alcoholic. At her dad's house she had been required to cook and clean for herself, her little sister, and her dad. Then when he was put in jail, Tabitha and her sister were sent to live with their mom.

Tabitha's mom, Julie, said she was afraid of being a teenager's parent—she just didn't know what to do since she had lived by herself for 10 years. Julie's frustrations and fears surfaced through rage. Tabitha was afraid to live with her mom, because she felt Julie had abandoned her 10 years earlier, and she feared being deserted again. She wanted to get good grades so her mom wouldn't get mad at her. Her fear of abandonment motivated her cheating in classes and the arguing with her mom.

> **Parent Power Point: Be alert to indications that your child is feeling anger because of the expectations you're placing on your teen.**

Tabitha expressed her anger in completely different ways than school gunmen. She and her mom got into counseling, and Julie began attending parenting classes. It was a rocky road for quite a while, and they both continue to work on their issues.

Unmet Needs

What is the reason for the degree of anger we see today in kids such as Tabitha? When they shoot their classmates, fight with others, blow up repeatedly at home, or cheat in classes, those activities ultimately make their lives more difficult. So why do teens get on, or stay on, such a path to destruction?

Their behavior is intentional. It fills an unmet need. When we see the purpose behind their actions, we can effectively deal with their anger. In order to find out what needs kids are trying to meet, we must know what those needs are. I have found that typically the reasons for anger stem from various types of unmet needs.

In his book *All I Really Need to Know I Learned in Kindergarten,* Robert Fulgham addresses basic rules for living successfully. For instance, regarding the way we treat others, he points out such necessary basics as sharing, not hitting, playing fair, learning to say we're sorry, and not taking things that belong to others. Some of his other points involve basic consideration, such as putting things back where they belong and cleaning up our own messes. Fulgham even points out lessons we learn in kindergarten on how to take care of ourselves, such as maintaining good health by washing our hands before we eat; taking naps or resting; developing a balanced life; finding wonder and noticing the little things, like watching a plant grow from a seed in a cup; and "When you go out into the world, watch out for traffic, hold hands, and stick together."[1]

Of course, this is a simplistic way of looking at needs, but we can see how it acknowledges some of our basic needs. If all of us would practice these rules, many of the reasons for anger would be nonexistent.

From a more sophisticated psychological model, Abraham Maslow developed what he called the "Hierarchy of Needs." Maslow supported humanistic psychology, and although I disagree with most of his philosophy, I do agree with his Hierarchy of Needs. His premise was that we are all motivated by unsatisfied needs and that certain lower needs must be taken care of before higher needs can be met. The diagram on the following page depicts Maslow's Hierarchy of Needs.

Maslow's model and the "kindergarten" model are ways to describe the needs we all have. I like summarizing the needs of kids today with the acronym "H.E.L.P."—Health, Environment, Love, Purpose. All these areas represent the cate-

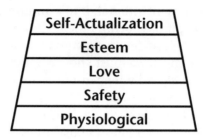

gories of needs in kids' lives. The most essential need, though, is in the area of health.

Health

Health involves our most basic needs, such as water, food, sleep, shelter, and so on. If those are not met, every other area of life is affected. Without clean water, disease from bacteria can cause severe health problems.

The lack of food causes hunger and impacts the ability to learn. With the new focus in education on standardized testing, schools find that they need to provide food and drinks for the kids before the testing or during a break in the testing. The number of students who don't eat breakfast or have inadequate meals at home is greater than most people realize. It's now generally accepted that empty stomachs produce lower test scores.

> Parent Power Point: Teens have specific nutritional needs, so check out what your teen is eating at school. Some schools let parents prepay for school lunches, which might prevent trips to the vending machine.

Another scenario regarding the need for food was evident in an elementary school where I taught. A boy kept stealing other students' lunches. After several disciplinary actions, we learned that his family ate only one meal of refried beans and tortillas per day. His single mom had six kids. The school started providing the boy with a lunch each day. With his need met, the stealing stopped.

Other kids could face a lack of sleep. Part of the reason Tabitha's grades dropped was because her mother's live-in boyfriend fought with her mother almost every night, so the quarreling kept Tabitha awake. No wonder she couldn't succeed in class—she was getting only three or four hours of sleep per night.

> Parent Power Point: **Many parents don't realize that teens actually need more sleep than younger kids—not less.**

Shelter is another need in kids' lives. At one school where I counseled, about 5 percent of our students lived in hotels in the red-light district. Some of their mothers were prostitutes who changed hotels weekly or monthly depending on how good the business was.

In another school, about 10 percent of our students lived in shacks with no glass in the windows. They were at the mercy of the weather and other threats, such as being robbed. How could they concentrate on their schoolwork after being robbed the night before? Other kids I've worked with have had the electricity shut off in their houses because bills weren't paid. How can we blame kids when some of the reasons for their anger result from their living conditions?

Water, food, sleep, and shelter give youth a feeling of safety and security. In *The Wizard of Oz*, Dorothy claimed, "There's no place like home." She longed to go home. However, today some kids would choose to stay in Oz instead of going home because of abusive situations at home. Some home situations are beyond the parents' control. However, most attempt to do the best they can with what they have. And many with meager resources are still able to make their dwelling into a home.

Environment

When we were young, the most influential people in our lives were probably our parents. Today young people are influenced by their environment—their cultural heritage, their neighborhood, their school and church, the influence of the media, and society as a whole. Some studies show that young people are more influenced by peers than parents. Kids most often mention that musicians and pro athletes are their role models. They're pressured to wear expensive sports shoes because the other kids at school have them. They're influenced to wear certain brands of clothes because "everyone at church wears them." Peer pressure is powerful.

As adults, we're shocked when sons or daughters come home with tattoos, piercings, or blue hair. Sometimes these startling changes in appearance are signs of rebellion, and sometimes they're just acts of curiosity or creative expressions. Sometimes they're attempts to get our attention.

> Parent Power Point: Strange clothing styles or funky hair may not be an indication that your teen is rebelling. It may simply mean your child is trying creative self-expression.
>
> If you suspect this is the case, determine if what your child is doing is really detrimental to health and well-being. If it's not, maybe the battle isn't worth fighting. Can you remember wearing clothes and hairstyles your parents didn't like?

Another factor influencing a teen's environment is the family's cultural values. More families are moving across the world than ever before. They often face conflicting cultural values between the country they left and the new one. Trouble arises when the kids want to shun their cultural heritage. Some cultures put much more value on time spent with family than on time spent with others. In some cultures parents have more control of their children's time and activities than in other cultures.

Our society has a powerful impact on our kids. So many expectations are tempting young people to bypass much of their childhood. They're forced to grow up too fast, and as a result, they lose a lot of their innocence. Many behaviors we're seeing in teens today are behaviors we previously expected from adults.

> Parent Power Point: **Help your teen realize that it's OK to go through life stages. Help your teen see that growing up is a process—not something that immediately happens when turning a certain age.**

Adolescents are confused about how they're supposed to act. The media says one thing, and the Church says another. Their peers may tell them to do something they know would be against their parents' values. That's why we have to pray and count on the solid foundation we've set in their lives. It's never too late to continue building upon that foundation. That foundation is love.

> Parent Power Point: **Don't be naive. Realize how your values are different from those held by your teen's peers. Learn about your child's culture. Look at teen magazines, movies, and television shows. Watch teens in the mall. Purposely take steps to help your teen understand your family's values and faith. Help your child learn to be discerning, and empower your teen to find and live out his or her own faith in society.**

Love

Many of our kids experience three types of love in their world:

1. I'll love you if you do this for me, or if you let me . . .
2. I love you because when I'm with you I'm in the popular crowd.

3. I love you no matter who you are or what you've done.

One of the few places kids receive the third kind of love is at home. Even though we know the influence society and their peers have on them, parents still have the lasting impact in their lives. Prov. 22:6 assures us that even though we can't see our impact yet, we are to "train a child in the way he should go, and when he is old he will not turn from it."

The most grounded and successful kids I've worked with in full-time ministry and in schools are those who have a parent or parents to love them. As a parent, you won't always do the right thing, but I believe God will take care of those situations that could cause them harm when we mistakenly use the wrong strategy in disciplining them. As long as we constantly seek His will regarding our kids and are willing to learn and grow in our parenting skills, God will take care of the rest. We'll make mistakes, but when we do, it's important that we remember to admit our mistakes to our children.

> **Parent Power Point: As long as we constantly seek God's will regarding our kids and are willing to learn and grow in our parenting skills, God will take care of the rest. After all, they're His kids too.**

Some of the most powerful times in my counseling office are when a parent who misunderstood something about a son or daughter apologizes to the teen. That does more for a kid than any words anyone else could ever say to them. Teens notice when their parents behave hypocritically. If we repeatedly discipline our teens for bad behaviors but then turn around and display those same behaviors, our teens naturally think, *That's not fair!* This builds anger in their lives.

There are times in life when adults legitimately live by a different set of rules than their children. When those things bother your children, explain what the difference is.

When you do make a mistake, such as losing your temper with your children, acknowledge your wrong actions to your children. When appropriate, ask your children for forgiveness. We must strive to model appropriate and good behavior to our children but must also be realistic about our failures. When we fail, we also need to model to our kids how to deal with it. Humility and willingness to be the first to admit we were wrong can melt a teen's angry heart.

Parents' relationships with their kids are ultimately the most important relationships they'll ever have beyond their relationships with God and their spouses. Teens' relationships with their parents will affect whom they marry and their relationships with their spouses.

> Parent Power Point: **We parents don't always make the best decisions when raising our kids. The point is not that we do everything right, but that our kids know we love them and that we try.**

When teens don't have a good relationship with their parents, they will seek to meet those needs through other people. Kids need to feel a sense of belonging, and they will keep looking until they find it. Even if they can get it from home, they still look for it from their peers. Young people need to belong to a group. If someone is shunned by a group in church or school, they'll keep looking until they find a group that will let them in. That's why gangs are so popular. They provide a sense of acceptance and belonging, even if their activities are destructive.

Once the need to feel accepted is met, teens are free to be themselves instead of feeling the need to put on masks. If they get into the wrong group by pretending to be something they're not, they'll have to maintain that persona the entire time they're a part of that group. That's why it's important for parents to present opportunities for them to get into situations in which they'll have contact with positive groups. Hopefully, with the love and acceptance we provide, they'll feel secure enough to face rejection and won't place such a high priority on being liked by others.

Love is a lifestyle. Some kids are tougher to love than others. If you're parenting a teen who is just like you, you will probably experience more conflicts. When we have a tough time loving our kids, we can pray for God to help us love them.

When I encounter difficult situations with students, I pray for God to help me see them through His eyes and to learn to love them. It has worked each time. Often He has showed me that I needed to let go of some expectations I had of them. I learned to love them just as they are—idiosyncrasies and all.

The greatest picture of God's love for us is the relationship between a parent and a child. If there is open communication, acceptance of who they are, a lack of judgmental attitudes, and security in the relationship, kids will grow up to love God and not be afraid to commit their lives to Him.

Some people have the impression that God is waiting for us to mess up so He can punish us. Jesus' example clarifies unconditional love for us. When the religious leaders confronted Jesus about the woman caught in adultery (see John 8:3-11), His attitude toward her was one not of judgment but of forgiveness. His reply to the religious leaders who brought her to Him is sobering: "If any one of you is without sin, let him be the first to throw a stone at her" (v. 7). After her accusers left, Jesus said to her, "Woman, where are they? Has no one condemned you?"

"No one, sir," she said.

"Then neither do I condemn you," Jesus declared. "Go now and leave your life of sin" (vv. 10-11).

That was unconditional love. Her actions could have brought serious consequences—even death. But when she left Jesus' presence, she felt encouraged, challenged, and forgiven.

When our kids leave our presence after disciplinary action, they should not feel humiliated. If they do, they'll be more likely to develop anger. Unconditional love will help us show our disappointment in their actions, not in them as persons. Once kids know they're loved, their futures appear brighter.

Purpose

Young people need a cause. They want to strive for something bigger than themselves. When they have the security that comes from their needs being met, they can give of themselves to help others.

Everyone has gifts and talents. In working with kids and parents on plans for after high school, I ask the students about their special talents. Most don't know. Their parents immediately chime in to say what they've seen in their children. When parents validate adolescents' gifts in that way, the teens brighten up and can see how those gifts relate to career areas they might be successful in—whether as homemaker, auto mechanic, attorney, or computer programmer.

> **Parent Power Point: Don't stay silent! Notice your teen's talents and accomplishments and applaud him or her in private and even in public when appropriate—and look for times when it's appropriate, such as in front of adults your teen respects.**

It's important for Christians to realize what their spiritual gifts are. See if your church has a spiritual gifts test you can take. It's so exciting to see how your natural abilities complement the spiritual gifts God has given you. When you're involved in work in which your natural gifts and spiritual gifts are being used, you experience immeasurable fulfillment. God has placed within all of us exactly what we need in order to fulfill the purpose He has for our lives.

God's purpose for you as a parent may seem discouraging at times. Even though there may be times you feel like giving up, you're making an incredible difference in your kids' lives. It may not seem like it at times, but hang in there.

Action Steps

1. Do your children have any unmet needs in the area of health or environment? If so, what are they?

2. Do you see any signs indicating that they're seeking to fill any unmet needs for love in inappropriate ways? How is this affecting them?
3. What are your children's gifts or talents? Tell them or write about them in a note saying that you appreciate those things about them.
4. Do you sense that your children have found a purpose for their lives? (It may not be their life purpose, but rather just something to strive for now.) If not, how can you help them explore that area?
5. In Isa. 55:8-9 God says, "My thoughts are not your thoughts, neither are your ways my ways, . . . As the heavens are higher than the earth, so are my ways higher than your ways and my thoughts than your thoughts." Write out a prayer for God to show you whether your children have any unmet needs that you're unaware of that could be the reasons for their anger, and ask God to reveal to them His vision for their lives.

4
The Cost of Anger

September 11, 2001, was the day of the worst terrorist attack on American soil. April 20, 1999, was the date of the Columbine High School shootings in Littleton, Colorado. Almost every person has in his or her memory the date of a family tragedy. Each event has a cost—not just for the perpetrators, but also for the victims and the surrounding society. Every type of anger, from yelling and slamming doors to ditching school to depression, has a cost. The price paid is usually never recovered and leaves a mark on all impacted by the event.

A Fatal Cost

One September evening Nathan drove down a highway at breakneck speed after fighting with his girlfriend. Another car swerved in front of him, trying to get to an exit ramp.

Nathan's anger escalated, and he followed the car and forced it off the road. The car rolled several times, killing one girl in the car and paralyzing the other, her sister. Nathan's impetuous rage forever changed his life and those of the sister and the two families.

When we're angry we don't usually explore all the implications of our anger. As parents, we can help our teens by teaching them the price they might have to pay for anger.

Parent Power Point: **The PRICE of anger usually involves consequences in these realms: Personal, Relational, Institutional/occupational, Civic, Emotional.**

Let's explore that price. Although Nathan seems like an extreme situation, no one ever expected his anger to escalate and lead to murder. You might want to share the illustration of Nathan with your own teens and let them expand on the results suggested below.

What price are all those involved paying for Nathan's split-second decision? Consider the following areas in each of their lives:

P—Personal
R—Relational
I—Institutional/occupational
C—Civic
E—Emotional

Personal

Nathan is paying a high personal price for his actions. He will be an old man when he's released from prison. His parents are paying a heavy personal price as well.

One young woman lost her life, and her sister, Cynthia, lost the life she had always known. As a quadriplegic, she will never again walk, feed herself, or enjoy most of the activities she loved.

Cynthia's family lost their precious daughter and now must learn to care for a quadriplegic daughter.

Relational

Nathan suffered the relational cost of his father's disowning him and his brother's refusal to speak to him. His mother visits him regularly in jail but spends sleepless nights worrying about him. Nathan lost his chance of having a relationship with his girlfriend and other friends, and his chances of enjoying a marriage are probably lessened since he could be 60 years old when released from prison.

Nathan's parents' relationship faltered under the weight of the stress. His family is often blamed for his actions. They don't attend many of the events they're invited to because of the questions and attitudes they face.

Cynthia lost her best friend: her sister. As a result of her paralysis, Cynthia will never bear children. Her loneliness makes the days seem to drag on forever.

Institutional/Occupational

Nathan's dream of going into engineering vaporized. His occupational aspirations are limited to training available in jail. His mother has missed a lot of work because she has not been feeling well since the tragedy. The exit ramp where the incident occurred is on her way to work. The constant reminder has been too much for her. She is considering looking for another job.

Cynthia won't be able to pursue her career goal of being a paramedic. After being in the hospital, she was moved to a rehabilitation center and is now learning new occupational skills—skills limited by her physical disabilities.

Civic

As an outstanding student, Nathan was in a mentoring program. He now had to figure out how to explain his mistake to the little boy he had mentored. He could not attend the state leadership conference as a delegate from the student government group at his school. He wondered if he could ever be a leader again. He wished he could tell his friends not to make the same mistake he did.

Nathan's dad resigned his board position for a local civic organization—everything had changed because of Nathan's anger. His mom resigned her Sunday School teaching position, afraid she could lead no one because she blamed herself for not correcting the anger in Nathan that led to this tragedy.

Emotional

Nathan is continually depressed, and his anger flares when his mother visits him. He won't tell her what life is like inside the jail. It's hard for her to visit him, but she knows she's his only lifeline to the outside world since his friends don't visit him. She has become withdrawn and faces recurring headaches. She still cries easily. Because her friends don't contact her as often as before, she faces the challenges of life alone. Her husband seems perpetually angry and has started drinking. He won't talk to his wife about Nathan and doesn't even ask about her visits to the prison.

Cynthia has been depressed and even thinks of suicide—although she couldn't attempt it alone since she is paralyzed. She often wishes she was the one who died in the wreck. She has recurring nightmares of the accident and her sister's screams, and can't imagine how she'll make it through life without being able to use her arms and legs.

Cynthia's parents are still dealing with their grief over their daughter's death, as well as trying to be strong and think of ways to cheer Cynthia. Her mother planned to go to a counselor when she had time, . . . but she has never been able to break away. Her father has been busy with details—insurance, plans to make the house wheelchair accessible, figuring how to cover the extra costs they're incurring from all the doctors' bills and other expenses revolving around their new lives. He keeps busy so he doesn't have to face his grief—afraid it will totally devastate him when he has to deal with it.

Others Impacted

It's crushing to see the impact on Nathan and Cynthia and their families by one split second of uncontrolled anger. Families are not the only ones impacted. Others on the periphery are also affected.

During the week after the Columbine tragedy and two days per week that summer, I counseled in elementary schools and the middle school that fed into Columbine, as well as at a crisis drop-in center set up for Columbine students and parents. The individuals I worked with were victims of the ripple effect of the explosive anger of the gunmen. And now the victims were dealing with their own anger. Those who dealt with their anger (or are still working on it) know it can be a long process. Others have lost hope of ever being freed from the memories and pain. Many turned to drugs or alcohol, and some even ended their lives. All the residual effects of the tragedy are a microcosm of the impact of anger on society as a whole.

The impact on one group that was often overlooked was the Columbine faculty and staff. Many of them risked their lives to run through the halls warning students or by hiding students. One of these heroes was Dave Sanders, the teacher who lost his life in the process. That caused the tragedy to hit closer to home for me, because I had coached with Dave when I was a student teacher at Columbine several years earlier. He was an incredible coach, and the players loved him dearly. He was just the type of person who would give his life to help others. Yet that doesn't take away his family's or students' grief.

Two days after the shooting, I was called to the elementary school where his wife, Linda, taught kindergartners. It was the first day the children were back in school. I'll never forget the tears of those kindergartners in her class who were asking questions they shouldn't have had to think about. It was difficult to see the grief of Linda's colleagues as they were forced to face the unthinkable for their friend. Then those teachers had to go into their classrooms and be strong for their students, many of whom had been in Linda's previous kindergarten classes.

The healing process for the Columbine faculty has been long. Fifteen months after the tragedy and heading into the new 2000-2001 school year, some of the staff members were in a meeting a week before school started. They had been warned that the fire alarms would be tested that day. The sound of the fire alarms had been changed from the particular sound they had made when many were hiding in the school for three hours with the alarms blaring.

But even with the warning and the change in the alarm's sound, the shrillness of the alarm traumatized one staff member to the point that she requested an immediate transfer to another school. She and others still had horrible flashbacks when the fire alarms went off. The staff member's request for a transfer was granted.

Many of the Columbine staff retired early or transferred to other schools because the tragedy impacted them so deeply. Although they wanted to stay at Columbine, the constant reminders and struggles with their own grief prevented them from being at their best for the students. As some moved to other schools, they asked their new principals to warn them before scheduling fire drills.

There are many residual effects of this tragedy that the general public is not aware of. And the same is true anytime we express our anger inappropriately.

The Cost to Society

As if the lists of costs to those impacted by tragedy weren't enough, we must not forget the cost to society as a whole. Health care and insurance expenses are impacted by the violence in our society. The costs involved with the September 11 tragedies are astronomical. The financial cost related to crime are creating a dilemma for society. In some states, building prisons and detention facilities have a higher priority than school funding because of the degree of the crime problem. And at the root of this violence and crime, anger is usually a key factor.

Kids Need Our Help

The cost of uncontrolled anger in our society is mind-boggling. What can we do to help? How can we make a dent in those amounts?

For starters, as we deal with our own children's anger, we can help them learn to harness it before it becomes uncontrollable. We can teach them appropriate ways to deal with their anger. As they learn to deal with anger in the small circumstances of life, it will help them face it in larger circumstances or will help them keep from letting little things—like a driver cutting them off—result in tragedy.

Here are some of the steps we can teach our children.

Appropriate Ways to Deal with Anger
- Pray for the person with whom you're angry.
- Remove yourself from the situation if your emotions are escalating so you can cool down before dealing with it.
- Talk with the person with whom you're angry as soon

as possible to try to resolve the issue. If you can't express yourself verbally because you get too emotional, write it out in a letter to the person.

- When confronting the other person, use "I" instead of "you" messages that could put him or her on the defensive. For example, "When you _____, I felt _____."
- Accept responsibility for your part of the problem.
- If the other person gets emotional, try to stay one or two levels calmer. Don't match his or her emotion. This will help de-escalate the situation.
- If you're afraid to confront the other person, use the "empty chair" scenario. Sit across from an empty chair and pretend the other person is sitting there. Then practice what you want to say.
- You can also role-play with another person. Pretend that person is the one with whom you have a problem, and practice what you want to say.
- If you can't resolve the situation immediately, the following things will help you get the anger out in safe ways:
  - Throw ice cubes at a brick wall as hard as you can.
  - Hit a pillow.
  - Scream into a pillow.
  - Exercise.
  - Journal: Set a timer for five minutes and write anything that comes to your mind about the situation. Don't edit your writing; let the thoughts flow freely. Don't worry about spelling or grammar.
  - Make a "God Bag": Get a small paper bag and write "God Bag" on it. On a piece of paper, write down situations or things that make you angry and put it in the bag as a symbol of giving it over to God.
  - Breathe: Take in a long slow breath while silently counting to 10. Hold it in to the count of 5, and then slowly exhale while counting to 10. Repeat several times.

- Listen to soothing music.
- Draw or color what you're feeling.
- Write a letter to the person with whom you're angry. When you're finished, rip it up and throw it away. (Don't send it to the person.)

In chapter 3 we looked at some reasons for anger, but something even deeper may be involved. Roots or seeds of anger (that sometimes can be traced through the generations) may exist that will take courage to delve into. But in order to honestly deal with anger and finally get to the bottom of the problem, we must face it. The very lives of our young people may be hanging in the balance. We must forge ahead.

Action Steps

1. What is your child's anger costing the child personally?
2. How are your child's relationships being affected by the anger?
3. Are there any institutional/occupational costs of your child's anger? If so, what are they?
4. What are the civic or emotional costs of your child's anger?
5. The Bible says in Gal. 6:7, "A man reaps what he sows." Write out a prayer asking God to help your child begin to see what anger is truly costing and how negative its impact is. Also, pray that your child will realize how much easier and better life will be with the anger controlled. Pray for wisdom throughout the process.

5
The Roots of Anger

"Sandy, we had to hospitalize Veronica last night because she was talking about killing herself again," Juanita, Veronica's mother, told me. I sighed. Within a span of six months, Veronica had been hospitalized twice for suicide attempts. Juanita cried, "I don't know what to do anymore. Will anyone ever be able to help her?"

Veronica had grown up in Afghanistan, where she was repeatedly raped and witnessed relatives being shot. Now at 17, she struggled with intense flashbacks at unexpected times.

One evening during a basketball game, a player from the other team shot the ball. Veronica jumped to rebound it as it bounced off the rim. With the ball slipping through her hands, she fell into a heap. The referee thought she was injured, so he called a time-out. Her coach ran to her. Veronica wasn't injured but was in tears from another flashback.

Veronica went to the locker room where her mom and I found her in a back corner curled up in the fetal position. As her mom wrapped her arms around her, Veronica's body trembled.

"When I jumped for the ball, I remembered one of the times I was raped," she explained. "All I could see and feel was that man on top of me,"

Those flashbacks occurred often. Once in the middle of a math test, Veronica smelled gunpowder and was back at a young age seeing her cousin shot by military guerrillas. For those who haven't been in similar situations, it's hard to fathom the hopelessness of living with such intrusions in daily life—not being able to erase them from the mind. They impact every aspect of life. The memories of those traumas in Veronica's life were affecting her life many years later. The roots of anger, if not dealt with, can cause a person's life to be blanketed with shame.

> Parent Power Point: Anger often stems from a root of shame in a teen's life. Guilt is feeling bad about something you've done, but shame is feeling you're intrinsically a bad person.

Shame

The roots of anger differ from the reasons for anger in that they stem from deep in the soul and typically can't be cured with a quick-fix formula. Shame, one of the most common roots of anger, is different from guilt. Guilt is feeling bad about something you've done, but shame is feeling that you're bad. If you've acted badly, you can apologize or make amends. If you see yourself as a bad person—someone who is intrinsically flawed—there seems to be no remedy. John Bradshaw says,

> In itself, shame is not bad. Shame is a normal human emotion. Shame tells us of our limits. Shame keeps us in our human boundaries, letting us know we can and will make mistakes, and that we need help. What I discovered was that shame as a healthy human emotion can be transformed into shame as a state of being. As a state of being, shame takes over one's whole identity. To have shame as an identity is to believe that one's being is flawed, that one is defective as a human being. Once shame is transformed into an identity, it becomes toxic and dehumanizing.[1]

Veronica experienced shame on a daily basis because of being raped. When I first met her, she would barely look me in the eye. She hung her head and talked almost in a whisper in her broken English. She had no self-confidence and didn't want to stand out in a crowd, so she did everything to keep from being noticed. She felt dirty and marked for life. Her feelings of shame influenced every part of her life and interactions with others.

Compass of Shame

Donald Nathanson in his book *Shame and Pride* developed the concept of the "compass of shame," which describes the four typical ways people respond to shaming situations: withdrawal, avoidance, attacking others, and attacking self.[2] It is diagramed below:

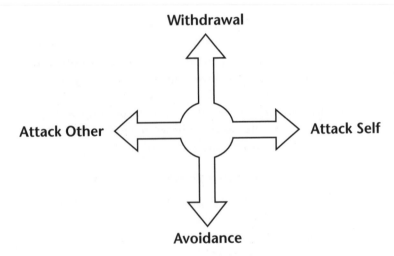

People who withdraw believe they can escape from an intolerable situation, and sometimes that withdrawal is swift and occasionally total.

Those who avoid find the experience of shame so toxic that they must prevent it at all costs. They engage in a number of strategies to reduce, minimize, shake off, or limit the effect. These types of people may abuse drugs or alcohol or go out of their way to distract attention away from what might bring them shame.

Others who find the helplessness and isolation of the first two categories intolerable want to place their shame under their own control by attacking themselves. They're willing to experience shame as long as others understand that they have done so voluntarily and with the intention of fostering a relationship with outsiders.

Those who attack others basically address their shame by believing, "Someone must be made lower than me." Almost every incident of bullying, graffiti, public vandalism, put-downs, ridicule, contempt, intentional public humiliation, and domestic violence can be traced to this style of dealing with shame.[3] Hence, unhealed shame issues lead to angry, aggressive behavior.

> Parent Power Point: Aggressive, angry behavior may mean your child is facing feelings of shame. Sometimes teens feeling shame abuse others to put someone else at a lower level than they feel they're at.

To understand more clearly whether your child struggles with shame issues, refer to the following chart to see if he or she is impacted by any of these areas of shame:

The Cognitive Phases of Shame

A. Matters of personal size, strength, ability, skill
("I am weak, incompetent, stupid.")

B. Dependence/independence
(Sense of helplessness.)

C. Competition
("I am a loser.")

D. Sense of self
("I am unique only to the extent that I am defective.")

E. Personal attractiveness
("I am ugly or deformed. My features make me
even more of a target of contempt.")

F. Sexuality
("There's something wrong with me sexually.")

G. Issues of seeing and being seen
(The urge to escape from the eyes before which we have been
exposed. The wish for a hole to open and swallow us.)

H. Wishes and fears about closeness
(The sense of being shunned from all humanity. A feeling
that one is unlovable. The wish to be left alone forever.)[4]

In looking back at Nathanson's "Compass of Shame,"
William Pollack's research in *Real Boys* would suggest that, in
general, boys probably have more of a tendency to react toward shame out of the avoidance and attacking others quad-
rants, while girls generally act out of the withdrawal and attacking self quadrant. Again, these are generalizations, and
exceptions always exist.

Some people propose that shame can also be a part of
generational sin. God said in Exod. 20:5 that the sins of fathers can affect their children to the third or fourth generations. Often we see this in families of alcoholics. An alcoholic
may have grown up with an alcoholic parent who was the
child of an alcoholic parent too. But the cycle can be broken.
God continues in the next verse in Exod. 20:6—"but showing
love to a thousand generations of those who love me and
keep my commandments."

So there is hope. Which would we prefer? It takes courage
to face the traumas that have caused such deep pain, but it's
worth it in the end.

> Parent Power Point: **By helping your child overcome
> an anger problem, you're also helping your family's
> future generations.**

Unresolved Trauma

Another root of anger is unresolved trauma. Recently my
school was forced to face a number of student suicides. All of
us felt heart-wrenching grief and pain. In the midst of helping students work through the grief of losing friends or classmates, a particular group stood out to me: many who didn't
even know the students who took their lives were overcome
with incredible amounts of grief too.

Parent Power Point: If your teen seems surprisingly affected and distraught by a societal tragedy—a tragedy that happened to someone he or she doesn't even know—this could be an indication that your child is dealing with some unresolved trauma in his or her own life.

One young man personified the impact that unresolved trauma can have on a person's life if it's not faced. This typically macho boy came into my office and said, "Ms. Austin, some of my friends said they're worried about me and told me I should come in to talk with you."

"Did you know any of the students, Mario?"

"No. That's why I don't understand why I'm so sad. I'm having trouble sleeping, and I don't feel like eating. I don't want to go to work. I called in sick yesterday. I just don't want to do anything."

"Have you ever felt like this before?"

"Yeah." A tear welled up in his eye. "My grandpa died when I was 10." The tear trickled down his cheek. "He was my best friend. We went fishing every week in the summers, and I could talk to him about anything. I haven't fished in five years."

More tears came. Brushing them away, he told me how he missed his grandfather and the great times they had shared.

"Have there been any other times you've felt like this, Mario?" He paused, then sighed.

"Yes, when my dog, Rocky, died when I was 8. My parents got him when I was born, so we grew up together. That was really hard too."

"That must have been tough to lose your dog and then your grandpa two years later."

"Yeah, I felt so alone, especially after Grandpa died. My two best friends were gone, and it's never been the same."

"I was sad," he said, then he quickly interjected, "but I didn't cry. When Rocky died, my dad said, 'Big boys don't cry.' Then my dad had left us by the time grandpa died, and I knew it would be OK to cry then, but I wanted to be strong for Mom since Grandpa was her dad."

Mario told me that instead of crying, he either played video games, sat with his mom and sister while they cried, or just played in his bedroom. "Eventually the sadness went away," Mario said, with tears filling his eyes again.

Obviously Mario's sadness still affected him more than five years later. He told me that during the time of the suicides, he began drinking alcohol more than usual. His friends had noted his sadness and in concern took him drinking "to get away from all the junk going on."

> **Parent Power Point: We can help our teens deal with anger by letting them feel it's OK to cry instead of being ashamed and trying to bottle up their feelings.**

We talked to Mario's mom, and she got him into counseling to deal with the effects of his past losses. He could finally release all those bottled up tears in a safe place, with no risk of being shamed for crying.

> **Parent Power Point: When our kids have unresolved issues regarding trauma or losses, their lives can be hindered as they hide that anger.**

When people have unresolved issues they have never dealt with regarding trauma or losses, their lives can be hindered for many years.

Unresolved trauma that's not grieved about can become a cancer that slowly drains the life out of us. When people have been stifled in the middle of the grief process, they can remain stuck at that point in their emotional growth until it's finally worked through.

Years ago a commercial for Meineke mufflers said, "Pay me now or pay me later." That's the case with anger, and it's never truer than in dealing with the grief process of trauma.

People who aren't able to cry or grieve appropriately allow it to build up for years. Typically it eventually comes out as depression, rage, or other dysfunctional behaviors.

> Parent Power Point: When teens don't grieve appropriately, the feelings don't go away; they build up and may eventually surface through depression, rage, or other dysfunctional behaviors.

Some people are afraid that if they let themselves cry, they may never stop—or if they let themselves get angry, they may lose control. That's why it's important to work through deep traumas with a trained professional. It's also important to understand the different stages of the grief process.

Elizabeth Kubler-Ross in her book *On Death and Dying* penned five stages of grief. Although her research dealt specifically with people who know they're dying, any kind of distressing situation may include these stages:

1. Denial and isolation—this includes shock and withdrawal.
2. Anger—at the person for inflicting the hurt (even if he or she is dead), at society, or at self. If not dealt with accordingly, the person may displace his or her anger onto innocent bystanders.
3. Bargaining—telling oneself, *If I or he had only . . . this might not have happened,* and so on.
4. Depression—a numbing feeling often coupled with anger and sadness.
5. Acceptance—when the sting of the pain subsides (there will most likely always be some pain associated with it) and reality hits and the loss is finally acknowledged.[5]

The stages can take a different amount of time for each person and can even come and go in cycles.

Some people who don't understand the grief process make comments such as "She should be over it by now," "He's a wimp," or "That happened years ago." Those comments can drive the pain deeper. If you're stuck in a stage for many months, you may need to seek help from a professional. It's also natural to revisit a stage once you thought you already passed through it—this often happens at the anniversaries of a loss (one month, one year, first Christmas following the loss, and so on).

> Parent Power Point: **If your teen seems stuck for months in one of the grief stages, consider seeking help from a professional.**

The grief that follows trauma may seem unbearable at times, but it's actually the healing process one must go through. If someone is stifled in a middle stage of the process and is not able to work through that stage, that person will struggle with that area throughout life until finally able to address it. For instance, some people who never dealt with their childhood abuse are forced to finally walk through the healing process at 40 years of age or so because they finally realize the root of their problem. Unresolved trauma can impact many areas of life and relationships.

Fear

Another root of anger that can impact life and relationships is fear, which comes in all shapes and sizes. Two fears I deal with the most in teenagers are the fear of abandonment and rejection and the fear of losing control.

> Parent Power Point: **The two fears teens face most are the fear of abandonment and rejection and the fear of losing control.**

Fear of Abandonment and Rejection

The fear of abandonment and rejection has many different faces. Divorce is one of the most common areas in which these fears are manifested. More than 65 percent of the children born in the last three years of the 20th century will reach the age of 18 not living with both of their biological parents.

With divorce reaching such rates, we need to understand how kids are affected by it so we can provide for the needs that may not be met in their lives. Often when kids have felt abandoned, they will assume the full responsibility for failure when any of their relationships break up. As a result, they can go on to make poor choices in future relationships and do everything they can to prevent people from leaving them again.

William Pollack did groundbreaking research on the pressures boys face in society in his book *Real Boys*. (For similar research on girls I encourage you to read Mary Pipher's book *Reviving Ophelia*.) Pollack's follow-up book *Real Boys' Voices* reveals the impact of divorce on boys and girls:

> For many years, America underestimated the effects of divorce on girls because young women tended to be "good" about divorce—they cooperated and did not complain. Over the years, however, studies have shown that divorce actually has had devastating long-term effects on girls, damage that we missed because of girls' outwardly calm and compliant behavior.
>
> With boys, we've observed how divorce seems to increase their outward misbehavior. We noticed that these boys seem to fail classes, skip school, start fights, and take drugs more often than those who have not experienced their parents' divorcing.[6]

> **Parent Power Point: If you've been through a divorce, don't be surprised if you see aggressive anger in your child—especially in boys. This is normal for teens of divorced families and can be an indication to you that your teen is still dealing with issues regarding the divorce.**

In cases in which a parent leaves with no prior notice and the child sees the parent leave, or the child comes home from school to find that the parent has left, that child will probably have abandonment or attachment issues.

According to James Garbarino, "Children who don't develop attachment have trouble making appropriate emotional connections. They have trouble with their own feelings and with the feelings of others. They often lack the emotional fundamentals for becoming a well-functioning member of society and are prone to become infected by whatever social poisons are around them. In short, they have trouble learning the basics of empathy, sympathy, and caring."[7]

> **Parent Power Point: If your child seems to have problems developing emotional connections, the teen may be dealing with an abandonment issue.**

Fear of Losing Control

Loss of control is another type of fear that can be a root of anger. This type of fear can occur when something has happened to dramatically change a person's life. The individual may try anything to gain back some semblance of control—no matter the cost. These teens become very controlling of everything and everyone around them.

> **Parent Power Point: Aggressive, controlling teens might be reacting to their fear of losing control—a common result of major life changes.**

Sheila Walsh is a beloved author and speaker. In her book *Honestly* she talks about how the quality of her life as an adult has been impacted by events in her early years.

"When I look at pictures of me as a little girl before my father's illness, my eyes are full of mischief. As a preschool child, I was a tomboy, fearless and full of life. My mother declares that she didn't sit down till I was five years old. As a child I adored my father. He understood my tomboy ways and gave me space to fly. At this stage of my life, anything seemed possible."

However, Sheila's whole secure world changed when a

blood clot destroyed part of her father's brain. Though at first he was allowed to stay at home with his family, he had gone from being a loving father to being a frightening man who even chased Sheila in anger with a fireplace poker.

"Dark storms blew through his mind—and our house," she recalls. "What I saw in his eyes in those darker moments, I will carry with me for years. I truly believed at a core level I was a bad person. How else could I explain why someone who loved me suddenly turned on me in rage?"

For the family's safety, her father was eventually taken out of the home. He died within a year. But the results lasted for years.

Life moved from safe to scary overnight. I—the younger daughter—fell from being invincible to having to protect myself at all costs. Don't let anyone inside, I would tell myself. Perhaps someone will see whatever it was that your daddy saw. Perhaps that person will leave—and you know how much that hurts.

My first taste of anger—from my father to me as a child—had affected my whole life. I would do anything I could to diffuse an angry situation. Angry words or tone of voice—spoken even by myself—seemed to me to signal something dramatic was about to happen. I never gave myself permission to be angry; when things happened in my life that I should have been angry about, I just stuffed the feelings down. . . . Occasionally, when I wasn't being vigilant, little bits [of repressed anger] would escape, leaking out in sudden outbursts or sarcasm.[8]

> **Parent Power Point: If your teen doesn't give permission to be angry personally, when things happen that should make one angry, your teen may suppress those feelings.**

Sheila lived for many years thinking she had to be perfect and be in control of everything in her life. She became a popular Christian singer and co-host of *The 700 Club* television program on the Christian Broadcasting Network. But her perfectionism nearly resulted in a mental breakdown.

Through Sheila's healing process, she came to understand why she struggled with always feeling she needed to measure up to what other people expected of her. She lost the control she had always worked so hard to maintain but got the help she needed. She now speaks to women all over the country about how they can be free of fear with God's intervention.

How do you know when your child needs to see a professional therapist or psychologist?

- When you need more help than your youth minister, school counselor, or pastor is able to provide—or when the severity of your child's anger is more than these leaders are qualified to work with.
- When you're afraid of your child.
- When you've lost control of your child.
- When your child seems "stuck" and is not "moving on" in the healing process.
- When nothing you've tried has worked.
- When your child is displaying dangerous behavior.
- When your child is threatening self harm or threatening to harm others.
- When your child's anger is the dominating issue in the family—the family has to walk on eggshells to avoid triggering anger, or the quality of your life is dependent on how your child is doing on any given day.

If the initial stages of shame, unresolved trauma, and fear are not healed, their roots can strangle our souls. The quality of every area of life may suffer. Those roots must be dug up and exposed. Our young people don't know how to do that on their own, and they need our help.

In the next chapter we'll discuss some helpful guidelines in addressing anger. Let's dig in.

Action Steps

1. Are there any signs of shame in your teen's behavior? If so, which ones?
2. Is there any generational sin (the same problems in the family for several generations) in your family? Describe them.
3. Has your teen faced any losses or traumas? How did your teen deal with them?
4. Do you see any evidence of fear in your teen? What type of fear is it, and what do you think is at the root of it?
5. The roots we have discussed in this chapter break God's heart, and He wants to bring healing. The Book of Joel in the Old Testament describes how locusts ravaged the Israelites' land, robbing them of so much. In response, God said, "I will give you back what you lost to the . . . locusts" (Joel 2:24, NLT). Your teen may have lost childlike innocence through losses or traumas. God can "repay" and restore that in many ways. He wants to bring healing to your child, you, and your family. As the parent, you can break the cycle of unresolved anger. It may take some time, though. Write out your prayer to God concerning all this.

6

Addressing Our Kids' Anger

"Jacob, how many times do I need to tell you? Clean your room!" Tiffany's face was bright red. This was the third time she had told Jacob to clean his room in an hour. Ignoring his mother, he just sat in the middle of his room playing a video game, radiating an air of sullenness.

Tiffany ripped the video game electrical cord from the wall. She screamed, "What am I supposed to do with you? You don't care about anything! All right—fine! If you don't want to clean your room, you can just go without lunch again."

Tiffany started sobbing and stomped out of the room, slamming his door. Jacob responded by throwing the joystick at the door with all his might. "Why can't she just leave me alone?" he muttered. "Always on my case!"

> Parent Power Tip: Bad times to deal with your kids' anger:
> While they're mad.
> While you're mad.

One of the most volatile issues for many parents is the issue of kids' cleaning their rooms. It seems when hormones start flooding a kid's body in puberty, they push the room-cleaning brain cells right out of their bodies. In their place comes an angry, defiant, "Make me!"

I wish there was an easy answer for this age-old dilemma, but there isn't. Yet there are some helpful ideas in dealing with the anger parents feel in this situation. Room cleaning isn't the focus—it's important only as it relates to parents addressing anger in their kids.

> **Parent Power Point:** When you're furious at your kid, try to keep the emotions in check—even though your child's goal seems to be pulling your strings to get your emotions bursting. When you lose it, the teenager ends up in control of the situation. Sometimes keeping emotions in check means walking away and telling the child, "I need some space, but we will deal with this later.

Whose Problem Is It Anyway?

In their book *Boundaries,* Henry Cloud and John Townsend share the experience of a couple's struggle with their 25-year-old son's irresponsibility and how to make it his problem, not theirs. They said to the parents, "He doesn't have a problem—you do. He can pretty much do whatever he wants—no problem. You pay, you fret, you worry, you plan, you exert energy to keep him going. He doesn't have a problem because you have taken it from him. Those things should be his problem, but as it now stands, they are yours."[1]

In the example of Jacob and Tiffany, did you notice whose emotions were escalating? Jacob was sitting playing the video game while Tiffany grew more and more infuriated. So whose problem was it? Who was more impacted by it? Tiffany.

Jacob didn't react until his mom stormed out of his room; actually his inaction was a reaction. His passive-aggressive behavior put him in control of the situation. To regain control, Tiffany must make the issue Jacob's problem instead of hers. We initially think it's Jacob's problem because it's his room that's messy. However, it didn't seem to bother Jacob much at all, but his mom was definitely upset about it. The solution to this situation is to make the messy room Jacob's problem.

Let's use this situation to demonstrate how parents can address a daughter's anger. You may think Tiffany's situation is a simplistic example, but with it we can make analogies about some of the more difficult circumstances you may have to confront. There are some steps you can follow in addressing your child's anger:

1. Acknowledge the problem.
2. Realize your part of the equation.
3. Seek help and support.
4. Determine what needs to change to make it the child's problem.
5. State the changes in expectations and the related consequences.
6. Implement the changes.
7. Give feedback and follow-up

Acknowledge the Problem

This is probably the easiest step of the process, but you may be the only one who acknowledges a problem. In Tiffany's example, the original concern is Jacob's messy room, but the more immediate problem becomes Jacob's ignoring his mother's request and his anger toward his mom. Tiffany knows there's a problem, but it doesn't seem that Jacob has realized it yet.

To address this issue, Tiffany needs to let Jacob know (1) his behavior is unacceptable and needs to change, (2) in the near future they'll sit down and talk about the changes that need to be made, and (3) he needs to start thinking about his part of the process.

Another part of acknowledging the problem is making a commitment to carry the process through to the end. You'll face times when you will need to be strong and follow through even when you don't feel like it or when it doesn't seem to make any difference. Prayer is the most vital aspect in confronting and harnessing anger. You'll need wisdom and discernment from God for the different types of situations that arise.

The following verse can be your prayer for your household: "If my people, who are called by my name, will humble themselves and pray and seek my face and turn from their wicked ways, then will I hear from heaven and will forgive their sins and will heal their land" (2 Chron. 7:14). God wants to help heal your home. As parents, the most humbling part is realizing the influence we play in our children's anger problems.

Realize Your Part of the Equation

This may be the toughest part of the process. We need to ask God to show us any part we've played in the development of our kid's anger problem. If we don't accept our responsibility, how can we expect our children to accept theirs?

Do you have an anger problem? Darryl DelHousaye of Scottsdale Bible Church in Scottsdale, Arizona, uses the analogy of a teacup, explaining that when you bump a teacup, whatever is in it comes out. When we get "bumped," what comes out? If our reactions are disproportionate to the situation, we probably have a problem. It's a warning signal that something needs our attention.

As we analyze our part of the equation, we must honestly evaluate how we handle our anger. If we have an anger problem, we need to work on it, too, or our kids will never hear a word we say to them. If at any point we realize we have inappropriately used our anger toward our kids (which has happened with all of us), then we need to apologize to them and ask them to forgive us. We can do this during any stage in the process. Pray for God to show you the best timing and approach. It can be one of the most powerful moments in life for you and your child.

The Bible talks about our responsibility in this: "Fathers, do not exasperate your children; instead, bring them up in the training and instruction of the Lord" (Eph. 6:4).

"If anyone causes one of these little ones who believe in me to sin, it would be better for him to be thrown into the sea with a large millstone tied around his neck" (Mark 9:42).

God is a forgiving God, and if we've missed the mark in this area, He is gracious and will forgive us. We need to be willing to change, and He will help us. He will help us find the resources for the support and help we need to deal with our issues and our children's issues.

> **Parent Power Point:** If we parents are dealing with anger in our own lives, we need to acknowledge this to our teens, or they'll never listen to anything we say. We can ask them to forgive us at any point during the process.

Seek Help and Support

To succeed on this journey of helping your child with his or her anger, you'll need help and support. You can go it alone, but with others by your side, your load will be lighter. You may feel it would be embarrassing to tell someone that you or your teen has an anger problem. You would be surprised to find out how many people struggle with this issue. You're not alone.

Maybe you can find a friend to read this book with you, and then you can learn together. Or consider asking the youth leader at your church if you could start a group for parents to read through the book together. You could read one chapter each week and then discuss the main points and the Action Steps. I encourage you to find someone to pray for you as you go through this process of dealing with your children's anger.

You may even know some parents whose kids are college-age or older who might be willing to walk with you through this time. If you have your own issues with anger, look for a spiritual leader in your church whom you respect, and ask him or her to hold you accountable. You may even want to seek professional help if you're concerned about the degree of your anger or want to explore its roots.

Parent Power Point: **Find someone who will walk with you through this time. And find someone to pray for your family.**

Determine How to Make It the Child's Problem

A lot of thought and prayer needs to go into how to make your child's anger his problem. Let's take the example of Jacob's messy room again. It's important to Tiffany that Jacob's room be clean.

In order to make his messy room Jacob's problem instead of Tiffany's, she can change some household procedures. In the past when Tiffany washed clothes, she went into Jacob's room and gathered his dirty clothes from the floor. She could change that by telling Jacob to start putting his dirty clothes into a basket beside the washer and dryer. Then when it's time to do laundry, if Jacob hasn't done his part, his clothes won't be washed. It probably won't be a big deal to him if he misses a couple of times, but eventually he'll feel the need to take responsibility for his own dirty clothes. This would make it his own problem.

Sometimes Tiffany makes Jacob's bed when the sheets and covers are on the floor. If she didn't do that, Jacob eventually would have to do something to get the sheets and blankets back on the bed. Also, for example, if he leaves dirty dishes from snacks on his floor, that poses a health hazard and becomes part of Tiffany's problem again. If he plans on going out with his friends that night, she could tell Jacob he can't leave until he puts his dishes in the dishwasher. If his friends have to wait for him, then it becomes his problem again.

Kids with belligerent behaviors turn these situations into a game of waiting you out. Then it becomes your problem again. For example, at my high school when some kids ditch classes, their parents choose to attend each class with them for a day. At first it's the parents' problem because it cuts into daily responsibilities, but in the first class it becomes the student's problem, because the teen is embarrassed for friends to see that parent there. The last thing high school kids want is Mom or Dad tagging along for a day.

When you encounter these difficult situations, you need the support network you formed in the last step. Call them. This can help you get another perspective. Also, if your teen is in school, let the staff know you're trying to work on your son's or daughter's anger or whatever other problem you are dealing with. Most teachers will, if they can, reinforce in their classroom what you're doing at home. If your teenager knows you're all working together on this, he or she will know it's important for all areas of life.

State Changes in Expectations and the Related Consequences

Perhaps without even realizing it, you've already stated the new expectations and consequences in conjunction with the previous step. Make sure the expectations and consequences are specific and clearly stated. Any vagueness will leave the issue open for all sorts of interpretation and cause more grounds for argument. Ask your child to repeat to you the expectations and consequences.

Let your kids know you're trying to improve your relationship with them. Reassure them of your love throughout the entire process. Listen to them. Ask them what they feel about how things have been with the old expectations. Validate their feelings and experiences. They may say they're mad that everything is changing. Tell them you can understand why they feel that way but that the changes are necessary to make the situation better for everyone. Tell them you want to help them learn how to take responsibility for their own actions.

Tiffany might also want to introduce the subject of self-talk to Jacob. We all engage in self-talk—what we say to ourselves during each day. She could ask Jacob what thoughts went through his mind when he got into trouble for not having his room clean. Were they encouraging or demeaning? When she changed the rules and his friends had to wait for him to put his dirty dishes away, what did he say to himself?

Then she could ask him if it was working for him. Were his actions producing the results he desired?

> **Parent Power Point: In dealing with expectations and anger, let your kids know you're trying to improve your relationship with them.**

Next Tiffany can ask Jacob what he could do differently. She could teach him to challenge his own thoughts. She could say she doesn't want him to be hearing those negative thoughts, either, but there are things we have to do all our lives that we don't enjoy—like having to stop at traffic lights or stop signs when we're in a hurry. Eventually we just have to follow the imposed rules for everyone's health and safety.

That type of situation could be a teachable moment for Jacob. It would force Jacob and his mother to communicate. At first they may not have a long conversation, but hopefully they will gradually get to that point. Communication is so important. Our kids want to talk to us; they just don't always know how to carry on a conversation. It's our job to teach and model good communication skills.

Implement the Changes

Let your kids know when the changes will take effect (give them plenty of notice—about a week if appropriate). Before they take effect, in the presence of everyone involved, make sure every person understands the new expectations and the consequences so they can ask questions for clarification. Tell the kids specifically how the consequences will be dealt with.

Give Feedback and Follow-Up

Consistency and fairness are the keys here. If an expectation is not met, check to see what the child's understanding of the expectation was. Make sure you remain in control of your emotions. If your kids have tried you in the past, they will at this point too. Expect them to offer a myriad of excuses. Calmly follow through with consequences.

If you feel you're beginning to lose your cool, tell them you don't want to respond to them in anger and that you'll deal with the situation after you cool down. Then get away from the situation—leave the room if you need to. When you've cooled down, deal with the problem as soon as possible. The Bible addresses this in Eph. 4:26—"'In your anger do not sin': Do not let the sun go down while you are still angry."

> **Parent Power Point: When you got in trouble growing up, did your mother ever say to you, "Just wait until your dad gets home," or "Go to your room, and I'll deal with you later"? Did you start dreading what was going to happen? Or has a boss or someone in authority over you ever said, "I need to see you in my office"? What went through your mind? Did you spend the next few moments wondering what you did wrong? Likewise, when you are losing control and you step away from the situation until you gain your composure, it causes your child to think about it too. This can be a good thing if it is done in the right way.**

In confronting your son or daughter, keep a few things in mind. If you can, pray before you confront your child. Treat your child with dignity, without name-calling or put-downs. When you follow through with the consequences, remember that your child will judge his self-worth by how you treat him. Validate your child's feelings. Ask her the reason for what she did—and listen carefully. Being confronted by a parent causes a child to feel very vulnerable. Handle it carefully.

I wish I could say that now your life will be free from out-of-control and angry situations, but we all know that won't happen. After you've followed all these steps in one situation, other situations will continue to arise.

Problems, conflict, and anger are a part of living. Therefore, we would do well to learn strategies to help prevent the escalation of anger. That's what we'll cover in the next chapter. We've come a long way.

> Parent Power Point: **Being confronted by a parent causes a child to feel very vulnerable. Handle it carefully.**

Action Steps

1. How do you handle your frustration with your teen?
2. List ways you may exacerbate your teen's anger.
3. What are some places or people you can go to for help and support as you begin addressing your child's anger problem? How and when will you pursue that avenue of help?
4. How can you make your teen's anger problem his instead of yours?
5. Many of your efforts in the past in dealing with your son's or daughter's anger may have been ineffective. In order to see the anger problem objectively or to approach the problem effectively, God wants to renew your mind so you can see the situation with new eyes. Rom. 12:2 says, "Do not conform any longer to the pattern of this world, but be transformed by the renewing of your mind." Write a prayer asking God to renew your mind.

7

Preventing the Escalation of Anger

The shrill ring of the telephone pierced the darkness of the crisp October night. "Sandy, I did it!" Heather's scream jolted me from my sleep, and I sprang to life.

"What happened?"

Excited, Heather replied, "I saw the way of escape this time—not right away, but I prayed, and God opened my eyes!"

This was big news, because the last time Heather missed seeing the way of escape, she was raped.

Six months earlier, Heather and her mom, Maria, had come to my office at the church. I was the youth director, and Heather was a new 10th grader in our youth group who had just moved to our city. The night before her family moved, Heather was date raped. Devastated, she entered counseling to work through the effects of the rape.

In the fall a boy from our high school asked Heather to homecoming. She came to me to find out how she could prepare mentally for the date because she had a lot of fears, and she didn't want to be raped again. I talked with Heather about a concept from 1 Cor. that I shared in youth group: "No temptation has seized you except what is common to man. And God is faithful; He will not let you be tempted beyond what you can bear. But when you are tempted, He will also provide a way out so that you can stand up under it" (10:13).

I told Heather that God often provides ways of escape, but we frequently don't see them. In explaining the concept, we talked about her rape to see if she could have escaped the situation. Heather said she and her date had gone to dinner and then a movie. After the movie, her date wanted to stop by a party before taking her home. She told him she didn't want to go to the party, but he said they would just go for a few minutes. On the way to the party, he stopped by a liquor store. She told him to take her home. He convinced her that he couldn't stop at the party without bringing something to drink.

Parent Power Point: Teach teens to look for ways to escape from bad situations.

When they got to the party, she wanted to stay in the car, but he talked her into going in because it was cold outside. When they got inside he went into the kitchen. He came out with an orange soda for her and a beer for himself. She took a few sips, and the next thing she knew, she woke up in the upstairs bedroom—she had been raped. She called her dad to pick her up.

In my office, while reviewing that date, Heather saw three opportunities she had missed to call her dad when she was concerned—at the theater, at the liquor store, and when she first got to the party. That knowledge empowered Heather for her homecoming date.

During the homecoming date, the young man wanted to stop at two parties after the dinner and dance. The entire time, Heather kept her eyes open for ways of escape should she need them, but she wasn't paranoid. The first party was OK, but at the second party almost everyone was drunk. She asked her date to take her home. He said he wanted to stay another 30 minutes and refused to take her home. She found a phone and called her dad.

Heather didn't know for sure if danger was ahead and was embarrassed to go home with her dad—but she felt the caution was worth it if it prevented her from more pain. She knew her date and his friends would probably never ask her to go out with them again, but she knew her body and mind were more important than their acceptance.

Six months earlier, when Heather first visited me, her

anger from the rape had escalated. Her mom was afraid Heather would become full of rage, sink into depression, or even begin acting out sexually because of the shame she felt. But Heather didn't want to stay in the condition she was in. She had the courage to face her circumstances and went through the right steps in the healing process to empower herself to live life instead of being robbed of it.

As she healed, Heather learned how to make smarter decisions in choosing the guys she dated. She was able to prevent her anger about the rape from building to the point of debilitating her for the rest of her life. She learned how to take care of her own needs.

Heather learned several important keys that prevented the escalation of her anger after the rape—a better understanding of boundaries, temperaments/personalities, and healthy conflict resolution. Volumes of books have been written on these topics, but let's touch briefly on them.

> **Boundaries are those love-lines we establish that say, "I'm sorry you're having a bad day, but you may not punish me for it."** —Patsy Clairmont

Boundaries

In chapter 6 we looked at an illustration from the book *Boundaries* to introduce the idea of making your children's problems theirs instead of yours. Boundaries are a misunderstood concept to a lot of people. Cloud and Townsend, the authors of *Boundaries,* give the example of a couple's boundary issues with their 25-year-old-son, who had problems with drugs and his ability to stay in school or find a job:

Look at it this way. It is as if he's your neighbor, who never waters his lawn. But whenever you turn on your sprinkler system, the water falls on his lawn. Your grass is turning brown and dying, but he looks down at his green grass and thinks to himself, "My yard is doing fine." That is how your son's life is. He doesn't study, or plan, or work, yet he has a nice place to live, plenty of money, and all the rights of a family member who is doing his part.

If you would define the property lines a little better, if you would fix the sprinkler system so that the water would fall on your lawn, and if he didn't water his own lawn, he would have to live in dirt. He might not like that after a while"[1]

That might have sounded cruel to the parents, but they finally realized that their "helping" was actually hurting their son. They had the best of intentions but were preventing him from having to face the consequences of his actions and the realities of life.

> **Parent Power Point: When we refuse to set boundaries for our children, we're actually hurting them and enabling them to continue in bad behavior.**

In her book *Mending Your Heart in a Broken World,* Patsy Clairmont writes, "Boundaries are those love-lines we establish that say, 'I'm sorry you're having a bad day, but you may not punish me for it.' There's a big difference between support and indulgence, but sometimes that line is hard to distinguish. Separating ourselves from others' hostility keeps us from absorbing their anger, which has the potential of setting a match to our own (and we all have some)."[2]

At one of my former schools, students were "using" Jenny because of her genuine caring heart. She was the manager for my volleyball team. She didn't have many friends, so being part of our team automatically gave her several "friends" she wouldn't have had otherwise. In her hunger for love, she reveled in any attention she could get. One day a girl on the team left her homework assignment at home. She asked Jenny to skip her class and drive her home to get her assignment. Jenny willingly did it. Some of the other girls in the school asked her to take them to a fast food restaurant each day for lunch because they didn't have a car.

Word got out that she was obliging, and more kids asked her for favors. She loved it because she thought she was gaining more friends. The straw that broke the camel's back was when Jenny had other lunch plans and some students asked if they could borrow her car to go to lunch. In Jenny's car they raced through the restaurant parking lot and hit another car—totaling both vehicles. We were shocked when we heard how far the situation had gotten out of hand. Jenny learned a hard lesson about boundaries.

In Cloud and Townsend's book, *Boundaries for Kids,* the authors state that there are three roles parents fill in their children's lives: guardian, manager, and source. The guardian role consists of protection and preservation for their kids in providing a safe environment. The manager role is one in which the parent makes sure things get done, such as reaching goals plus meeting demands and expectations. As the source, parents provide the necessary resources their children need for growing—food, shelter, supplies, love, spiritual growth, wisdom, support, and knowledge.[3]

These are all building blocks from which to build an accurate understanding of healthy boundaries. If these foundational needs are met in children's lives, they will be better equipped to deal with anger problems. The next key for preventing the escalation of anger is a clear understanding of how your child's temperament or personality contributes to the anger issues.

Temperament/Personality

One of the biggest influences in how we process anger is our temperament or personality style. Earlier I mentioned that often parents have more conflicts with a child who has a similar personality. That is sometimes because the weaknesses we see in ourselves are the same ones we see in the child, and that is where the conflicts arise. It is important for you to know your own personality type as well as that of each family member.

Knowing the personality types can give you valuable information as to the strengths, weaknesses, and relating styles of each person in your family. That can give you insight into why they do what they do and where you'll probably encounter conflicts between the different personality styles. We can improve relationships and diminish conflicts simply by understanding the reasons a certain family member seems like a thorn in our flesh.

> Parent Power Point: **Knowing the personality types of your family members can give you valuable information about their strengths, weaknesses, and communication styles.**

A lot of theories of personalities have been developed through the ages. There are many personality tests you can take to find out this information. The Myers-Briggs Type Indicator is the industry standard and a test that many people are familiar with.

Isabel Myers and Kathryn Briggs devised a questionnaire to identify different personality types, distinguishing that people's personalities are made up of preferences in handling life situations. After answering the questions, people can find out their personality preferences in four categories. The four categories are as follows:

E—Extraversion (Expressive) versus I—Introversion (Reserved)

S—Sensing (Observant) versus N—Intuition (Introspective)

T—Thinking (Tough-minded) versus F—Feeling (Friendly)

J—Judging (Scheduling) versus P—Perceiving (Probing)[4]

The results of the Myers-Briggs Type Indicator would reveal four letters to indicate the person's personality type. For example, ESTJ, INFP, and so on.

After much study, David Keirsey made further observations in that the combinations of how people scored on the preferences determined 16 general temperament types. He then narrowed those 16 types to four general categories. He found the combination of those two categories revealed the most about the person's temperament and was able to delineate those types through a test he named the Keirsey Temperament Sorter II. His four categories followed by their four subcategories are as follows. (The initials coincide with the ones used in the Myers-Briggs Type Indicator):

SJ—"The Guardians"—characterized as "Security Seeking," which are further broken down into Supervisors, Inspectors, Providers, and Protectors.

SP—"The Artisans," "Sensation Seekers"—Promoters, Crafters, Performers, and Composers.

NT—"The Rationals," "Knowledge Seekers"—Fieldmarshals, Masterminds, Inventors, and Architects.

NF—"The Idealists," "Identity Seeking"—Teachers, Counselors, Champions, Healers.[5]

Hippocrates was the first to suggest that there are four basic personality types. He named them Sanguine, Choleric, Melancholy, and Phlegmatic. Tim LaHaye came up with a spiritual point of view for Hippocrates' four main personality categories in his book *Spirit-Controlled Temperaments*. He breaks down his descriptions of the temperaments into the following:

Sanguine—warm, buoyant, lively, enjoying, and the life of the party.

Choleric—hot, quick, active, practical, and strong-willed, and very independent.

Melancholy—analytical, self-sacrificing, gifted, perfectionist, and very sensitive.

Phlegmatic—calm, cool, slow, easy-going, and well-balanced.[6]

Studying personality types will help you know that sometimes a teenager isn't being defiant but is simply staying true to his or her basic personality. For instance, you may feel your child withdraws from you because she is angry, or maybe you think he is suppressing anger because he looks upset. However, if you know your child has tendencies toward being melancholic, you might find that the withdrawal is simply a tendency of these thinkers. And meeting you with a stoic or sullen expression may not mean the teen is angry —perhaps the teen's mind is just elsewhere, on other things, as melancholics tend to do.

Or, as an example on the other hand, if we have a melancholic teen, because these personality types tend to be sensitive and sometimes overly-sensitive, we need to realize that we might say something matter-of-factly that the teen will take personally and get angry about.

Saying "I Love You"

Another aspect of personality that we need to note when we're trying to love our kids is to realize we may not speak the same language. Often I hear parents say, "I don't understand why he thinks I don't love him. I give him presents and do special things for him."

In *The Five Love Languages of Children,* Gary Chapman points out that we all can be loved in five ways, but we have preferences according to our personalities. The five love languages are physical touch, affirmative words, gifts, acts of service, and quality time.[7]

For instance, maybe your teen feels loved the most when you give hugs or other occasional touches. But maybe you're not much of a toucher—maybe you feel loved when people buy you gifts, and thus you buy your teen gifts to express your love. If the teen feels loved most by being touched, your teen will not realize your love until you start giving those hugs and literal pats on the back.

If we love others through the wrong methods, they won't be impacted until we understand their love language and love them in that way.

> **Parent Power Point: To insure that our teens feel loved, we need to learn their "love language" and meet their needs in that way.**

Pouring love on someone in his or her love language will hit the mark every time. When we miss the target, it can cause conflict and misunderstandings in relationships.

Healthy Conflict Resolution

One area regarding the prevention of anger escalation is the concept of healthy conflict resolution. Children learn to resolve conflict in the way they see modeled in their homes, primarily by their parents. If the parent yells and screams, the child will learn to do the same. Likewise, if the parents suppress their emotions, the child will learn to do the same. However, if parents have good anger management skills, their children will gradually learn to follow.

We can use some strategies in mediating conflicts or resolving disagreements. When a problem exists between two people—let's use the example of siblings—you can use the following steps in the acronym "RESOLVED":

R—Reach an Agreement. Ask if they are both willing to work it out. Don't proceed with both children if both will not agree to resolve the conflict. If only one is willing to talk about it, talk with that child.

E—Expectations. Each child will have a chance to tell his or her side of the problem. The disagreeing parties will speak one at a time and cannot interrupt the other person.

No put-downs or name-calling. Each should use "I" messages to express how he or she feels or what is wanted or needed from the other child. Deal only with one issue or problem at a time.

S—Share. Have each child repeat, without interruption, what each one heard the other child say.

O—Offer. Offer clarifications of misunderstandings that may need to be cleared up.

L—List Other Points. Ask for any other points that need to be made.

V—Voice Ideas for a Solution. Each child shares ideas for a solution.

E—Explain the Mutual Agreement. Check for a mutual agreement on a solution.

D—Determine to Get Along. Ask if they can both accept the solution. They need to agree to get along even if it means staying out of each other's way for a while.

Don't force them to say, "I'm sorry." They may still have some hurt feelings that need to be worked out. Ask them if they both will agree to begin working on forgiving each other. Forgiveness is a process that often takes longer to complete but starts with an act of the will.

For conflict mediation when the conflict is between you and your child, you can use the following example as steps:

1. Don't match your child's emotion. If your child begins to yell, stay at least one level lower in intensity. If you aren't escalating, your child likely won't either. Don't get into a shouting match. Model the behavior you desire from your child. Try to stay in control. If necessary, back off if you need time to cool down, but set a time to discuss it.

2. Take a deep breath. This will help you gain your composure and think about what to do next.

3. If you don't know, ask why your child is angry. Listen carefully. Acknowledge and validate the feelings—don't discount them or say "You shouldn't feel that way," "You're taking it too personally," and so on. Ask questions for clarification. Use "I" messages. As parents, we need to make sure we don't jump too quickly to a conclusion or assumption.

4. Ask what can be done to improve the situation. Acknowledge your child's ideas, and don't discount them even if they're completely off the wall. Talk your child through them, helping determine what might happen as a result of these ideas.

5. Come to a mutual decision on a solution. Check for understanding on your child's part too. The child may not agree with your solution, but as parents we're still the responsible ones.

6. Finish with some kind of affirmation. Commend your child for working on a solution. Assure your child of your love. If your child originally got in trouble because of doing something wrong, emphasize that it was a bad choice and that he or she is not a bad person. Don't label your child as "bad"—that has a shaming effect. When we blow

it, we must apologize for not responding appropriately and tell how we would like to handle it in the future.

Parent Power Point: **Don't label kids as "bad" when they get into trouble—simply emphasize that they made wrong choices.**

We can clearly see that as adults we have a tremendous amount of responsibility in implementing boundaries, understanding personality/temperaments, and modeling healthy conflict resolution. This may feel overwhelming, so we need to know how to take care of ourselves during the process. Next, we'll take a look at parent survival skills to help prevent us from losing our minds in the midst of it all.

Action Steps

1. List the ways in which your teen could benefit from understanding the ways of escape mentioned in 1 Cor. 10:13.
2. Write about any areas in your relationship with your teen in which you need to establish healthier boundaries. What are the new boundaries that need to be established?
3. Write down what you think is your child's love language. In what ways could your teen's love language and personality type play a role in your teen's anger problem?
4. What are some areas that you need to improve for healthy conflict resolution in your family?
5. In Zech. 4:6 the Bible says, "'Not by might nor by power, but by my Spirit,' says the Lord Almighty." That's the key for how to handle the times when your child's anger begins to escalate. Ask God for His help and wisdom in how to work through those times, so you won't try to work it out through your own ways.

8

Parent Survival Skills

A year ago J. D. was driving too fast on a neighborhood road. His Suburban ran out of control and hit five other cars. One man was thrown from his vehicle and died.

J. D. was in one of the most intensive academic programs in the country at a nearby high school. His computer skills gave him the potential to earn twice the salary many people make. But now he's in a youth detention facility for three years because of his actions last year.

About two months ago J. D.'s mom, Dinah, came to me regarding another incident. A youngster had hit another student, inflicting serious injury. Dinah said, "With everything I've been through with J. D. in the last year, I know some of what that boy's mother is going through. If you think it would help for me to talk to her, I'd be willing to do that."

At that point Dinah was awaiting her son's sentencing hearing, but amid her own pain, she was concerned for another mother. She personifies 2 Cor. 1:3-4: "Praise be to the God and Father of our Lord Jesus Christ, the Father of compassion and the God of all comfort, who comforts us in all our troubles, so that we can comfort those in any trouble with the comfort we ourselves have received from God."

Parenting is the toughest job in the world! No job is more demanding. A special license is required for driving a car, getting married, or even fishing, but not for parenting. Parents are expected to take a tiny crying baby and turn it into a law-abiding citizen, scholar, all-star athlete, child prodigy, "Mother Theresa," and "Billy Graham." In the next week, your parenting will probably include many of the following:

Restoring hopes

Relieving fears

Drying tears
Mediating conflicts
Taming bullies
Building-up confidence
Teaching life lessons
Inspiring dreams
Igniting smiles
Renewing peace
Carpooling
Making meals
Washing clothes
Cleaning house
Paying bills

Are you tired yet? As a parent you're truly a miracle worker. I know the frustrations you experience with not being able
to do the things you really want to do. Your dreams of why
you wanted to become a parent in the first place have become lost in the mire of trying to survive daily life.

How many times a week do you wake up and think of
your to-do list, then find at the end of the day that you
haven't been able to accomplish even one of those things?
Unexpected emergencies, drop-in visitors or calls, and house-
work piling up can consume every waking moment. Yet you
keep trying to reach out to your children. You spend untold
hours trying to make a shred of difference in their lives.

For those times you couldn't sleep because you were worrying about how your kid will handle that situation at school
the next day; for those times when you were misunderstood
when trying to help; for the times you wanted to yell back at
your child but didn't; for the times your child asked impossible questions; for talking with your stubborn child even
though you knew it probably wouldn't get you anywhere; for
the times you needed to make tough decisions your children
wouldn't understand; for the times you felt like pulling your
hair out; for the countless things you do each day that go unnoticed—thank you! And bless you for continuing to learn
and grow as a parent.

But what about you? Does your cup feel empty after so freely pouring your life into your family? We need to remember to take care of ourselves, because no one else will. Addressing your own needs will keep your cup full so you can continue to give. It's necessary if you are to survive. Survival involves four areas of our lives: our relationship with God, family, others, and ourselves.

Parent Power Point: We can most effectively meet our kids' needs when we've taken steps to make sure our own needs are fulfilled.

Relationship with God

God created us for relationship with himself. In *Your God Is Too Small,* J. B. Phillips' words ring true:

The trouble with many people today is that they have not found a God big enough for modern needs. While their experience of life has grown in a score of directions, and their mental horizons have been expanded to the point of bewilderment by world events and by scientific discoveries, their ideas of God have remained largely static. Many men and women are living, often with inner dissatisfaction, without any faith in God at all. This is not because they are particularly wicked or selfish or, as the old-fashioned would say, "godless," but that they have not found with their adult minds a God big enough to "account for" life, big enough to "fit in with" the new scientific age, big enough to command their highest admiration and respect, and consequently their willing cooperation.[1]

In another Christian classic, *The Christian's Secret of a Happy Life,* Hannah Whitall Smith states very clearly how society often views Christians: "You Christians seem to have a religion that makes you miserable. You are like a man with a headache. He does not want to get rid of his head, but it hurts him to keep it. You cannot expect outsiders to seek very earnestly for something so uncomfortable."[2]

Often our views of God are tarnished by other people. I remember a couple of sayings I heard growing up that relate to this: "It's not the Christian message that's so hard to believe —it's the messenger [Christians]." Also, "If you were put on trial for being a Christian, would there be enough evidence to convict you?"

How do you view God? Is your relationship with God all you want it to be? Do you read the promises of God in the Bible and think they must apply to everyone else but you? Have you been hurt by other Christians? Were you disillusioned by church "rules" you were told to live by? Maybe a tragedy happened in your life, and you wonder where God was or why He allowed it to happen. At times we endure struggles as a result of our decisions or others' decisions, and many questions remain unanswered.

Dinah says she has a lot of "yes, buts" with her son's situation. Her son's detention center is in a city an hour away from his home. She knows God will take care of her son there, but as a mother, she still worries. She knows her son will be able to further his education there, but will it help him get where he wants to go? Dinah's faith is being stretched to the limits in having to trust God with her son's well-being.

God wants to touch your heart and heal your hurts. He's big enough to handle your questions. Don't be afraid to ask Him. He'll always answer our questions, but sometimes not in the way we expect. He'll answer with, yes, no, or wait. His silence means "Wait." Don't be afraid to admit if you're angry with God—He already knows what's in your heart. He won't be shocked or disappointed. He gave you that emotion to show you when there's something wrong.

One day when I was working out, a man was running around the track, and his primary-age daughter was riding her bike on the outskirts of the track. The father warned the girl to stay away from a little ravine nearby. What did she do? Of course—she got dangerously close to it. The dirt gave way underneath, and both the girl and the bike tumbled into the ravine.

The father ran over to her. She was bleeding from the scrapes on her knees and elbows. He hugged her and then said, "I told you to stay away from the ravine." She pushed him away and started hitting his legs in anger and embarrassment while crying. As her energy drained, her hitting slowed down. Then, exhausted, she fell against her father's legs and wept silently. "That's OK, Honey," he said. "I still love you. I'll always love you."

Tears flooded my eyes. I had recently lost a dream job. Through that scene the Lord had impressed on me, "Sandy, I know you're deeply hurt. I know you have questions. I know you're afraid. I know you feel alone. Come to Me. Flail and scream like that little girl. Ask your questions. Get mad at Me. Crawl into My arms."

I left the track and drove to my favorite place at the foot of a mountain. No one was around, so I began to pour out my heart to God. I yelled and screamed and cried. Then I felt God's peace wash over me. The verse in Jer. 29:11 came to me: "'I know the plans I have for you,' declares the LORD, 'plans to prosper you and not to harm you, plans to give you hope and a future.'"

Looking back at what God impressed on me then, and seeing what's happened in my life since then, I can honestly say I'm thankful God closed that door. He has led me on to other things, and I see how He prepared me for what I have experienced with the Columbine tragedy and in my counseling career. Jer. 29:11 has come true in my life.

Ask God to reveal to you what His love is really like. He is reaching out to you in those painful places that may have impacted your views of Him. Do whatever you need to get to the bottom of your issues with God.

Renewing the Mind

As a result of everything that bombards us in this world, we can have a lot of distortions about God or life. The Bible says in Rom. 12:2, "Do not conform any longer to the pattern of this world, but be transformed by the renewing of your mind. Then you will be able to test and approve what God's will is— His good, pleasing and perfect will."

Ask God to reveal if you have any wrong concepts of Him, and ask Him to renew your mind. He doesn't think the way we do.

God has said, "My thoughts are not your thoughts, neither are your ways my ways, . . . As the heavens are higher than the earth, so are my ways higher than your ways and my thoughts than your thoughts" (Isa. 55:8-9).

When you became a Christian, you became a "new creation," as stated in 2 Cor. 5:17. As you grow in your walk with God, more of His attributes should become part of your life. Those attributes are also called the fruit of the Spirit as presented in Gal. 5:22-23—"The fruit of the Spirit is love, joy, peace, patience, kindness, goodness, faithfulness, gentleness and self-control."

Before you begin reading the Bible, ask God to show you what He wants you to know about Him. "Then you will call upon me and come and pray to me, and I will listen to you. You will seek me and find me when you seek me with all your heart" (Jer. 29:12-13).

Relationships with Family

Family relationships can be a source of support or a drain. If you're married, your relationship with your spouse is important during trying times with your children. As you know, sometimes kids will pit one parent against the other. That's why parents must communicate. It's important to support each other. Try to spend time together—just the two of you. Go on dates again.

Keep building your relationship with your spouse, because you can tend to blame each other for your child's problems. If your relationship and communication is strong, you will withstand the onslaught of doubts. It's important that any roles the parents are playing in the child's problem are addressed, though.

Family problems involve many factors. If couples start

blaming each other, they may not be able to weather the storm. If problems exist between you and your spouse, get help immediately. You need each other to make it through the tough times.

I have some friends whose only daughter killed herself many years ago. As a result, this couple faced a rough time in their marriage, but now their relationship is stronger than ever. Now they spearhead an organization that reaches out to loved ones of those who have committed suicide.

If you're a single parent, you may feel you have to fill in as both the mother and father figures for your children. Get whatever support you need. If the absent parent is not available for visits, that can make the situation more difficult. For example, if you're a single mom, try to make sure your children have access to men who can be good role models for them. Ask some of those men if they would be willing to be a part of your children's lives in some way. One man at my church takes a single mother's boy out to athletic events, movies, and other places. His influence is making up for some of the things the boy is missing from his absent father. The mother is relieved and grateful for the help.

Another survival skill is protecting your family's calendar. Try to say no to extra activities that can crowd your schedule and add stress to your life. Outside activities and friendships are great, but not when you're frantically trying to attend all the activities, or when the hectic pace results in arguments and stress. Family meals can provide quality time to establish relationships between family members.

The performance trap can be a vicious cycle of "keeping up with the Joneses." If we push our kids to do more and be better, they might think they don't measure up. This can cause more distress in a family.

Extended family can help in difficult times too. After her son's accident, Dinah received invaluable help from her sister and mother. Her sister knew Dinah might not be able to remember all the information during the legal meetings and hearings. She went with Dinah to each meeting and took copious notes for Dinah to review later. Dinah's mother stayed home and prayed. When she went to one trial and brought Dinah's wheelchair-bound brother, their presence provided moral support and relieved pressure. Dinah's niece also volunteered to do housecleaning.

Relationship with Others

Time for relationships with others may be at a premium during some stages of parenting. If you can establish a support network of others who are in your parenting stage, it can be a great encouragement to you.

During Dinah's difficult time, she found encouragement as her church provided meals and emotional and prayer support. The school personnel was understanding with J. D. and his schoolwork assignments. They also would not let the media come on campus to hound J. D. or his brother. Coworkers of Dinah and her husband provided food and time off for the court appearances. Dinah saved all the cards from friends and loved ones and stacked them on the kitchen counter. They were a source of encouragement when the pressure mounted. In some of those cards the senders had enclosed a check to help cover some of the extra expenses.

Relationship with Self

A key factor in our emotional survival is knowing what we need. Often as a parent your needs go unmet because you're helping everyone else. So the first thing is to assess your own needs.

What recharges your energy? Some find strength in times of solitude. Sometimes it's not possible for you to get away by yourself, so you need to break away for 10 minutes to have a cup of coffee or snuggle up with a good book. Or you might be energized by a walk or exercise. Those are ways to take care of yourself.

During the Columbine crisis, a mother of one of my students was stressed when she came to school to help her daughter with an art project. The mom had been cooped up at home with her family for several days after the school shootings, so she was on call 24/7. I told her to do something she loved, so she went home to read and take a hot bath. When she came back to school later, she was ready to give again. We need those times of refreshing.

When there are problems in your family, one of your greatest survival skills is to get help for yourself even if no one else in your family wants it. This is an area in which many have trouble because they have grown up thinking that anything they do for themselves is selfish. But if we have unmet needs, we won't be able to help our kids. As we examined our teens' basic needs in chapter 3, we see that we have those same needs as adults. Getting our own needs met is not selfish—it's necessary for survival.

During the difficult times, we have to honor our needs, too. A big part of that is letting the people around you know what needs you have. This takes courage. Often people tell you to let them know if you need anything. Write those names down, and when a need arises, look at the list to see who might be able to help you, and give them a call.

Another survival skill is the ability to ask questions to get your needs met. Dinah had to ask some tough questions. But that knowledge empowered her to know what to expect and how to handle what was coming up. Write your questions down so you don't forget to get the answers you need.

When you've done everything you can to survive through building your relationship with God, family, others, and yourself, you'll feel strengthened and have the support you need to face most situations.

Action Steps

1. Write out anything that may be hindering you in your relationship with God.
2. What areas of family relationships do you need to take a closer look at and why?
3. Do you have a relationship with someone outside your family that's a support and encouragement to you? Call or spend some time with that person to recharge your energy.

4. What is one way you can take care of yourself or pamper yourself this week?

5. Jesus states in Matt. 11:28-30, "Come to me, all you who are weary and burdened, and I will give you rest. Take my yoke upon you and learn from me, for I am gentle and humble in heart, and you will find rest for your souls. For my yoke is easy and my burden is light." Write a prayer asking God to show you how to take His yoke upon you and rest in Him.

9

Pitfalls to Avoid

Everyone was shocked to hear that Andy had killed himself—maybe everyone except me.

Andy had played basketball at a rival high school in our school district. His older brothers were good players, but Andy was the best athlete. His dad, Art, started coaching him in middle school when he saw his raw talent. Art seemed to live his dreams through Andy, pushing him year-round to train to become the best basketball player in the state.

Andy did become the best basketball player in the state. The media followed him, and some of the top colleges were recruiting him.

In his senior year Andy was the leading scorer in the state. He missed game-winning free throws in two games that, according to Art, cost his team the games. Andy noticed that Art didn't mention the other missed shots in the game. Andy's team was guaranteed a spot in the state tournament, and the league championship was the next stop on the way.

In the league championship game, Andy missed game-winning free throws again. Everyone said it was because his dad made him so nervous. Art yelled at him all the way into the locker room and all the way home. Andy couldn't handle another week of Art yelling at him until the next game. He killed himself that night. Now he doesn't have to worry about missing any more free throws.

Andy's story is heartbreaking. His dad wanted the best for him, but at what price? I found out later that Art was a second-string football player in high school and college. Sometimes parents who were frustrated with their own childhood try to live out their dreams through their own kids. And that can lead to anger in a teen's life.

Top Ten List of Pitfalls Parents Can Get Dragged Into

Art's situation is just one of many pitfalls parents can fall into while raising their children. We fall into some of them by our own ignorance and are pulled into others by our kids' behaviors. Again, awareness is the key. The following 10 pitfalls aren't listed in any certain order, but I believe the No. 1 entry is probably the biggest problem for parents in dealing with kids. So let's begin with No. 10.

The No. 10 Pitfall Parents Need to Avoid: "So You Don't Like My Blue Hair?"

It almost gets humorous at school each week to see what new hairstyle or hair color will show up in the halls. You name it—I've seen it. At first I didn't know what to say. I've found that kids want me to acknowledge it, though. I don't need to say I like it if I don't. Typically my comments are, "Wow—that's the brightest blue I've ever seen." "What made you choose green this week?" "Now that pink doesn't match your purse."

These types of comments make the kids smile. For the ones that grease their hair into a pointed Mohawk style, I often say, "Can I touch that?" or "How do you get it to stay up like that all day?" Then they proceed to tell me all about it.

I know it's easy for me to have that attitude since they're not my kids. But most kids who have done that type of thing are either trying to get a reaction from their parents, trying to get back at their parents, or just doing it out of curiosity or creative expression.

Several times I have known kids who wanted to "royally" get at their parents, as they would say, who dyed their hair before an important event in their parent's life. The best way I've seen this situation handled was when the parent took the teenager anyway. The parents were embarrassed, but their kids knew that tactic wouldn't work anymore. The old term of "reverse psychology" works with this scenario most of the time. If a parent does not react in extreme emotion but lets the son or daughter know how disappointed he or she is, that will often work. The color will eventually rinse or fade out, or the bizarre cut will grow out too. Remember: choose your battles carefully and prayerfully.

Piercings and tattoos are a similar issue. I believe they are a fad and will begin to disappear soon. I believe some of the piercings are for shock value. When the kids get old enough to work, that alleviates a lot of the problems with piercings and unconventional hairstyles, because bizarre appearance limits their job options. I tell kids who are thinking of getting piercings, "What will your future spouse think?" If that doesn't work, I ask "How is that going to look on you when you're 70?"

If kids want a tattoo, some parents let them get a little one on their ankle or arm to satisfy the urge. If you do that, I recommend you go with them. Some parents tell their kids that as long as the kids live in their house, they can't do that. That will work sometimes, but what if they do it anyway? Then you have another problem on your hands. This is a tough area to deal with.

> Parent Power Point: **Realize that appearances are only skin deep. Our teens are so much more than what meets the eye—something we need to be reminded of when the blue hair surfaces!**

The No. 9 Pitfall Parents Need to Avoid: Favoritism

Favoritism can cause deep hurt in children's lives. As I mentioned earlier, some children are more difficult to love than others. Even if this is true, parents must not be lured into this pitfall. I knew of one mom who had four children and always took the same child with her when she went shopping or to get coffee. The others knew she enjoyed being with that sibling more than the rest.

Sometimes you favor the one who's most like you or the least like you. Sometimes divorced parents dislike the child most who reminds them of their former spouse. I've also observed that if a child has a special need—physical, mental or emotional—sometimes that child is either favored or shunned. In some families the most talented child is favored.

Unfortunately, the children who are not favored often spend their entire lives trying to earn the approval of the parent who shunned them.

Favoritism can also cause pain for the favored child. Sometimes the other children gang up on the favored child when the parent isn't around. The story of Joseph in the Old Testament tells what can happen in that scenario (Gen. 37—50).

> Parent Power Point: **Some kids are tougher to love than others, but that may mean they need our love even more than those who are easy to love.**

The No. 8 Pitfall Parents Need to Avoid: Inconsistent Discipline

When we discussed boundaries in chapter 6, we discussed discipline at some length. The problem with setting boundaries is that once we set them, we need to be consistent in following through. The verses that come to mind are "He who spares the rod hates his son, but he who loves him is careful to discipline him" (Prov. 13:24) and "Train a child in the way he should go, and when he is old he will not turn from it" (Prov. 22:6).

Many other verses in the Bible refer to discipline. The key is how we administer discipline. If we do it out of our own anger, it will be wrong and often too harsh. It's important to remember that we need to cool down before we administer discipline.

Another problem is that when we're tired, we often want to take the easy way out and say to ourselves, "Just this one time I'll pretend I didn't hear that or see that." If we're tired or don't want to deal with a discipline situation at the moment, we can tell the child that we saw what happened and we will deal with it later. (If we say that, we need to make sure we follow up—maybe write it down so we don't forget—because the child will be expecting it).

And a key point to remember with discipline is to make sure we don't label our child as a "bad" kid. We need to emphasize that the action or choice was inappropriate, wrong, or bad, but that it doesn't make the child "bad."

> **Parent Power Point: The key to effective discipline is how we administer it. If we blow up in anger or make threats we don't follow through on, our teens take us less seriously.**

The No. 7 Pitfall Parents Need to Avoid: Being a "Helicopter" Parent

I'll tell you a secret from the world of education. A word is used to describe parents who are always hovering around their students at school—"helicopter" parent.

Don't get me wrong. Many parents volunteer their time at the school and are vital to the school environment. The problem is not the parents' desire to be involved in their child's life; the problem comes when they're so controlling that they do everything for their kids to the point that the students don't have to take responsibility for their actions. If a teen has a problem with another student, it's the parent who calls. If there's a problem with a teacher, we hear from the parent. If there is a problem with a homework assignment, the parent checks into it.

In such scenarios, the student does not learn the skills he or she needs to deal with problems. School is a laboratory for what kids will face in "the real world." If possible, the student should deal with the other student, the teacher, or the assignment whenever a problem arises. If a student doesn't feel comfortable with that, as a counselor I'll practice with the student on how to approach the person, what to say, and so on. Most other counselors will also help in that way.

At times, parents do need to step in and help. They just need to do it judiciously—not as a regular course of action.

How Can School Counselors Help You with Your Angry Child?

- They can be an adult voice in your child's life when your child begins pulling away from you and won't listen to you. Many times, kids will listen to what other adults say more than what their parents say—even though both adults are saying the same thing.
- They can help teach your child anger management steps.
- They can facilitate an intervention meeting between you and your child to address issues related to the anger. (They cannot meet with you on a weekly basis because of their caseload. If that type of counseling is necessary, they will give you information on resources outside of school that you can pursue.)
- They can be a liaison with teachers to let them know you are working on your child's anger problem and let the teachers know how they can reinforce what you are addressing with your student.
- They can conduct conflict mediations between your child and another student in the case of bullying problems.
- They can work to help bring about a resolution if there is a conflict between your child and a teacher or student.
- They can teach you and your child effective conflict resolution skills.
- They can help keep your son or daughter accountable to take responsibility for his or her actions.
- They can make your student feel valued and validated by another adult in the student's life.
- They can put you in touch with other resources to help you as you deal with your child's anger.

Please remember the national caseload average for school counselors is one counselor to every 561 students (according to the American School Counselor Association). So your school counselor will do everything he or she can do to help you and your child, but the counselor's efforts may be limited by time constraints. That's when they'll refer you to other community resources.

The policy at my school is that when a problem or misunderstanding exists, the person must first go to that person to try to work it out. If that doesn't solve it, then the student can go to someone in authority to get help. The Bible supports this theory: Jesus said, "If your brother sins against you, go and show him his fault, just between the two of you. If he listens to you, you have won your brother over. But if he will not listen, take one or two others along, so that every matter may be established by the testimony of two or three witnesses" (Matt. 18:15-16).

When I was young I was very shy. When people came to our door, if I couldn't run out of the living room, I would hide behind the sofa. As I got older, if I needed to call a store to find out if they had a product, I asked my mom to make the call. When I got into seventh grade, she made me start making those calls myself. I was deathly afraid, but as I persevered I learned the skills needed to feel comfortable making my own calls. I needed this skill to survive in the real world.

> Parent Power Point: **Parents who are over-involved in their kids' lives hinder their kids as much as parents who aren't involved enough.**

The No. 6 Pitfall Parents Need to Avoid: Living Our Lives Through Our Kids

During my 13 years of coaching high school sports, I often saw situations similar to that of Art and Andy. Parents yelled at their kids about their performance when a game was over. I tried to talk to those parents, but they rarely accepted what I said. Kids feel bad enough when they make a mistake—they don't need everyone else reminding them of it.

Those parents would argue that they were just trying to teach their child a lesson while it was fresh on her mind. The problem is not that they wanted to teach the child a lesson. Rather, it was the way they approached their teen that made the difference. If the approach is condemning, demeaning, or humiliating, the kids usually don't hear a word that is being said. Anger builds in those teens. Yes, they may suppress it because they don't dare yell back at their parents, but it eventually comes out in other ways.

Of the different girls I coached who dealt with a parent like that, some started behaving in ways to get back at that parent. One girl started dating a boy her parents disliked. When she was forbidden from that, she started hanging around with a rough crowd and smoking. One dyed her hair pink, while another became very bitter. One girl began to foul out early in each game while another kept getting injured—maybe then they could avoid the mistakes in the game that would cause their fathers to yell at them. I was the most concerned about another girl who withdrew and became very depressed.

The problem of parents demeaning their children in the athletic realm has come to be known as the "frustrated jock syndrome." It is very dangerous to try to live out our dreams through our kids. It is more important that we support our children's dreams rather than forcing ours upon them.

> Parent Power Point: It's more important that we support our children's dreams rather than forcing our dreams upon them.

The No. 5 Pitfall Parents Need to Avoid: Expecting Our Kids to Meet Our Social Needs

One way to keep disappointments you'll have with your children from impacting you so heavily is to make sure your whole life is not wrapped up in them. I'm not encouraging you to neglect your children, but you do need to have some other activities and relationships in your life. The parent-child relationship is one-sided: you're always giving.

I like the illustration of our lives as a bucket. We keep dipping our water out to all those around us, but we need to have our bucket replenished too. Think about all your relationships.

Do you have any relationships that have an equal give-and-take ratio in which you pour out to them but they also pour back to you? If most of your relationships are ones in which you're dipping out all the time, pray that God would bring some friends into your life that will give back to you too.

You may be saying, "That's a great idea, but who will take care of the kids while I'm developing friendships?" If you're married, have your spouse watch the kids while you spend an hour or two with friends. It's always so special to hear of husbands who watch the kids for a weekend while their wives get to go to a women's conference.

If you're a single parent, form a group of single parents and go out once a month. Each month have two people babysit all the kids while the others go out together. Rotate each month. (Or maybe you can find some relatives or other friends to watch the kids so you can all go out together.)

Also, if you're married, continue to develop your friendship with your spouse. As suggested earlier, have date nights. Also it's important to remember that the different sexes have different concepts of what friendship is all about. According to Dee Brestin in *Friendships of Women,* men's friendships consist mainly of doing an activity together like playing a game of golf. Women, on the other hand, just like to spend time together—they could spend hours over coffee just talking and talking.[1] So be aware of that when you're thinking about what to do on a date.

> Parent Power Point: **Our kids are in our lives for a limited time. We need to be there for them but also to have lives of our own.**

Divorced parents need to be careful to not turn a child into a surrogate spouse. Often if a divorced man or woman has a child of the opposite sex, they can tend to begin treating that child as a "spouse" in some ways. They can begin depending on them for things that only another adult should provide for them, including the emotional realm.

For example, a boy can feel the pressure to become "the man of the house." Yes, he can help with chores around the house that your husband used to do, but be careful, because you may tend to give him more responsibility than he can handle.

And men sometimes put unfair expectations on their daughters to do the cleaning, cooking, taking care of the other children, and so on. Please be careful of this. Many kids develop bitterness because they've been expected to fill in for their absent parent. Yes, in a divorce situation, everyone needs to chip in and pick up the slack in the duties of the absent parent, but as adults the main responsibility is ours.

Also, parents who are lonely may tend to treat their kids like peers to fill their need to talk to someone about their problems. This can confuse a child and cause him or her to either unhealthily cling to the parent (sometimes parenting the parent) or to avoid the parent. Teens who have been placed in this situation can end up being angry about losing their childhood.

> Parent Power Point: As our kids mature and start the road to adulthood, we need to remember that we're still their parents. We can't be their best friends. While they're in our homes under our authority, they're still our children. Later, when they're grown and gone, we can focus more on being buddies and building somewhat of a peer relationship.

The No. 4 Pitfall Parents Need to Avoid: Thinking That Suppressing Anger Is OK

People deal with anger in various ways, but one of the most dangerous ways is to suppress it. Sometimes these individuals do such a great job of looking all right on the surface that it comes as a shock when they go off the deep end.

Such people become that way if they think it's bad to be angry, if they don't feel it's safe to let their feelings out, or if they want to keep peace in the relationship at any cost.

Do you remember Mario in chapter 5, who never dealt with his grief from losing his grandpa and dog? He suppressed his anger. This type of person often expresses anger in ways that aren't easily noticed—by drinking, taking illegal drugs, cutting themselves, being depressed, developing eating disorders, and so on. Sometimes this person is afraid that if he gets mad, he will completely lose control, or if she starts crying it will be impossible to stop. Or the person blows up one day and everyone is shocked and makes comments like "Where on earth did that come from?" because they never saw that person angry before.

Here's a visual illustration to use with people who suppress anger:

Let's say you have a plastic bottle of Pepsi and drop it on the ground. If you open it immediately, it will spew all over. But if you open it a little to let some pressure out, then close it immediately, it won't spew out. If you continue to do that until all the pressure is released, you'll be able to drink it without it spewing all over you.

Help teens see that if they deal with their anger a little at a time, they'll be able to handle it and won't be overwhelmed by it. It's important that they know anger is a natural response to many situations. How they deal with it will make the difference. The best way to show them is by the way *you* deal with anger in front of them.

> **Parent Power Point: Help teens see that if they deal with their anger a little at a time, they'll be able to handle it and won't be overwhelmed by it.**

The No. 3 Pitfall Parents Need to Avoid: Wrong Expectations

Setting expectations for our children either too high or too low can set them up for failure. If we set our expectations so high that our teens can rarely meet them, despair may cause them to quit trying. If our expectations are too low, our children won't be challenged by their goals and may fall into complacency.

One thing is certain: kids strive for their parents' love all their lives. The most important thing you can do for your children is to let them know you love them just as they are.

Often our view of how God sees us is based on how we feel our parents see us. Sometimes parents are more worried about what others think of them than what's best for their children.

It's important not to compare your kids with each other. Celebrate their differences, and let them dream their own dreams. If your kids want to be in music and you hate music, don't discourage them. Don't try to squeeze your kids into a mold you have for them.

Many persons end up in careers they dislike because their parents pressured them into that career path. Let kids explore their interests and determine what they want to do with their lives.

The No. 2 Pitfall Parents Need to Avoid: Giving Up on Your Kids

Perseverance is the key to enduring this journey. We must hang in there and not give up on our teen. If we do, we can lose him or her for life. I can't think of anything more devastating than feeling your parents have given up on you.

> Parent Power Point: **If you give up on your child, you may lose that child permanently.**

As I mentioned earlier, those who never felt their parents' acceptance can spend their whole lives striving for it in other ways. Where else can they get the unconditional love they're supposed to get from their parents? We know it's from God, but teenagers often don't go to Him because their ideas of parents are projected onto God. I think the heart of a child whose parent has given up on him or her must be the toughest heart to penetrate.

If by any chance you have done that with your child, it will take time, but you can repair the breech. Seek help, and seek God. Just ask Him, and He'll come to you and mend your heart first. Then perhaps the relationship with your child can be mended as well.

Now—could we have a drum roll, please?

The No. 1 Pitfall Parents Need to Avoid: Getting Caught in the Drama Triangle

If I had a nickel for every triangular friendship I've dealt with throughout my years in counseling and education, I would be a rich woman. Whenever three are in a relationship, usually problems occur if not all participants are aware of the dynamics involved.

Under stressful situations, two people may recruit a third person into the relationship to reduce the anxiety and gain stability. This is called triangulation. Although triangulation may lessen the emotional tension between the two people, the underlying conflict is not addressed, and in the long run the situation worsens. If a couple has unresolved and intense conflicts, for instance, they may focus their attention on a problematic son. Instead of fighting with each other, they're temporarily distracted by riveting their attention on their son. Yet their basic conflict remains unresolved. Once the child's problem is resolved or he leaves home, they no longer have him to balance their system. The couple often resumes fighting or may even file for divorce, because their differences and conflicts were never resolved.[2]

Psychology has a theory called the "Drama Triangle," which was conceptualized by Steve Karpman. This theory maintains that in any relationship there can be someone who acts as a persecutor, a rescuer, or a victim.

The Drama Triangle shows the dramatic roles that people act-out in daily life that are unstable, unsatisfactory, repeated, emotionally competitive, and generate misery and discomfort for both people, sooner or later. The switching that occurs between the roles generates the drama and the painful feelings that occur when people have hidden agendas, secrets, and then manipulate for dysfunctional personal advantage.[3]

Let me give you an example of how this works. A mother and daughter are at the mall. The daughter wants to show her mother a $150 pair of shoes she spotted last week when she was at the mall with her friends. She says, "Mom, I gotta have those." Her mother responds, "I don't think so. The shoes you have are fine. We can't afford $150 for a pair of shoes no matter how cool you think they are."

She frowns, "Why not?" At this point, she begins to pull her mother into the Drama Triangle. When her mother explains again, she retorts, "You're so mean, you never let me have anything I like. All my friends' parents buy them these shoes." In essence, she lets her mother know, "By not buying me these shoes, you're being a lousy parent." What an effective tool in attacking a parent!

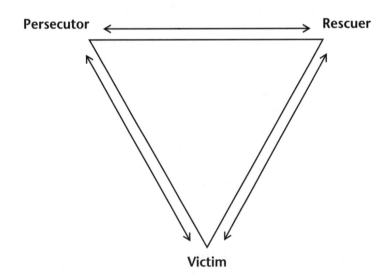

Persecutor ⟷ Rescuer

Victim

If you're not strong or are embarrassed or feel the good old parental guilt she's imposing on you, you may say, "OK—I'll get them for you for your birthday, but that's all you're getting for your birthday, and you can't have them until then."

In this situation, the daughter started as the victim but quickly switched to the persecutor when she didn't get her way. The diagram[4] on page 110 depicts the concept.

- **PERSECUTORS:** "I'm OK—you're not OK." They find fault in others, are critical and often unpleasant, and feel inadequate underneath. Their leadership style is using threats, orders, and rigidity, which can be loud or quiet. They sometimes appear as a bully and often use shame and blame in their interaction.
- **RESCUERS:** "I'm OK—you're not OK, so I'll save you." They always work hard to help others. They're characteristically extremely busy and tired from taking care of others. They often have physical complaints and are often angry underneath, lonely, and don't have a "life" of their own. They are martyrs and use guilt, shame, or blame.
- **VICTIMS:** "I'm not OK—you're OK." They are very needy, do less than their share of the work, and won't respond, won't reach out, won't take a stand. They simulate compliance, they are "supersensitive," and they'll not take no for an answer.[5]

The Drama Triangle begins when a person switches from one role to the other. In the situation in the mall, everything was going fine until the girl switched into the persecutor role.

Before, while the girl was in the victim role, the mother was explaining why she couldn't have the shoes. Could you feel a switch in emotion when the girl said, "You're so mean—you never let me have anything I like." She knew her mom would be embarrassed by that comment or be afraid that she was a "bad" parent.

The only way out of the Drama Triangle is to become detached—emotionally or physically. When we do that, we'll be perceived as the persecutor. In the earlier situation, instead of getting angry and walking away or giving in to her daughter, the mother could say in a calm voice, "I'm sorry you feel that way, Honey, but you can't have the shoes. We can talk about it later."

When the child sees she can't pull her mother into the Drama Triangle, she'll eventually stop.

There are some things we need to remember about the Drama Triangle. It begins when one person switches to another role, because it knocks others off balance. Everyone has a primary role he or she typically operates out of and a secondary role he or she moves into. The role we're least familiar with is the one that will catch us off guard and send us into the Drama Triangle.

> Parent Power Point: **Teens often move from the role of victim into the mode of persecutor during an encounter. This sudden switch of roles can cause the parent to lose balance and be pulled into a Drama Triangle.**

It's important to understand all the roles to see which one the other person switches into. If you can begin to recognize when this is happening, you'll be able to prevent yourself from being pulled into the role that will allow them to get their way. The only way to get out of the Drama Triangle is to detach.

Also, it's important to know that "Two people cannot stay in the same role for very long. People unconsciously change roles in the Drama Triangle to maintain their illusion of power. If you change roles on purpose—as a procedure—you can control yourself and minimize the damage to both of you when the other person gets stuck in the drama and manipulation to maintain power."[6]

Understanding the Drama Triangle can empower us in our relationships with teens. Roles are learned early in childhood and generally remain with us throughout our adult lives. In whatever realm of influence you find yourself, you will see the Drama Triangle played out—at home, church, work, community organizations, and so on. Your awareness can prevent you from being pulled into it and can save you a lot of heartache. Passing this understanding on to our children will do the same for them.

Power is often the motivating force that pulls people into the Drama Triangle and the other pitfalls we have discussed in this chapter. Understanding these pitfalls will help to prevent us from making some mistakes that can debilitate us or our children for years.

We made it through the top 10 list. Next we'll explore some anger issues as they're related to church. They're some of the reasons people have given up on having anything to do with church. Fasten your seat belt—it may be a rough ride.

Action Steps

1. Which is the main pitfall to which you most easily succumb?
2. Why do you think that's the case?
3. Write out how you can prepare yourself for the next time you face that situation.
4. Who can you talk to about this pitfall, and what are some questions you can ask that will help you diligently work to overcome this area?
5. James 1:5 says, "If any of you lacks wisdom, he should ask God, who gives generously to all without finding fault, and it will be given to him." Write a prayer asking God for the wisdom to see the pitfalls and to learn to avoid falling into them in the future.

10

Anger Issues Unique to the Church

Some anger issues exist that are not necessarily unique to the church—but what *is* unique is the way the church deals with them. The anger issues listed in this chapter are reasons teens and others have given me for not going to church. One of the biggest problems in the church is denial of problems, because many think they need to put on a facade that everything's OK.

In psychology circles there is a widely known illustration that depicts a dysfunctional family (a family with unhealthy patterns of relating). When a problem exists in the family, often it's not acknowledged, and everyone pretends it's not there.

It's as if an elephant is in the living room. Everyone walks around it, cleans around it, and so on, but no one acknowledges its presence. Before they can get the elephant out of the house, they have to acknowledge that it's there. We've already discussed how each person has to acknowledge the problem and how it affects all members of the family.

The following story is about a high school friend of mine. When she needed the support of her church the most, her church failed her. Denial can be deadly.

Pam called me one night because she had seen my name in her daughter Shauna's college address book. She asked if I had been in touch with Shauna since we had graduated from high school and had gone our separate ways. I admitted that the last time I had seen Shauna was before Christmas vacation.

"Shauna passed away last night, and I thought you would want to know that," Pam informed me. She said she needed to make a lot of other calls, so she cut our conversation short.

I felt as if someone had just punched me in the stomach. I started to cry.

Shauna and I had grown up in the same high school. We both played on the basketball team. I found out she was a Christian, and we went to the Christian group on campus. We hung out together and talked about the guys we were interested in, school, homework, and lots of other things. She became my best friend. We graduated from high school and hung out at the recreation center a lot during the summer. One afternoon a couple of days before we both were to head out to different colleges, we went for lunch, and she poured her heart out to me.

"Sandy, I need to tell you something I've kept hidden for a long time. My dad has been molesting me for the last four years. I don't know what to do." Shauna tried to compose herself. "I told my pastor last week, but he said I must be mistaken because my dad is such a good Christian man."

I was stunned and speechless. The pastor drove Shauna's pain deeper because he didn't believe her. The abuse plus this injury was the root of Shauna's anger. She told me as much as she could handle without making a scene at the restaurant. It was the local hangout, so we were repeatedly interrupted. Before we knew it, two hours had flown by, and I had to leave for a weekend retreat.

All weekend I couldn't get Shauna off my mind. When I got home, we talked for a couple hours. The next day we both left for our separate colleges. Shauna was excited to be able to get away from her dad.

With the excitement of being new college students, we were both very busy. We didn't get to see each other much, but we often talked on the phone. Shauna wanted to see a counselor about the abuse. She didn't think her parents would pay for one, so she started seeing one at the college. The counselor wasn't a Christian, and in one of their first sessions he said, "How can you still believe in God since He let that happen to you?"

Shauna started getting confused. She thought, *God was what got me through those years, but that's a good question—why did He let that happen to me?* She started to sink into despair.

Her roommates started experimenting with drugs, and in her depression Shauna didn't stand up to the peer pressure. So she joined in with them. I found out about the drugs the next time I called, so that weekend I drove the three hours to see her. She looked very depressed.

We spent long hours talking, hanging out together, and going to some movies. I encouraged her to try to see another counselor. I dreaded returning to my college and leaving Shauna. I was really concerned about her.

Shauna tried to make an appointment with another counselor, but the rest of the ones at the school were booked. The next weekend was the weekend before finals. I drove to her school again, and we studied all weekend. After finals she was heading home to Texas. She was scared to see her dad, but she said she would keep busy with other things.

While on vacation, we talked a couple times on the phone, and she said she was doing OK. Then the day after Christmas, I got Pam's call. Pam said Shauna and her dad got into an argument after the Christmas dinner. Pam didn't say it was a suicide, but I knew it was.

All these years later I still miss Shauna. I have never been the same. Shauna was one of those kids who dreamed of a bright future. She had been a leader in her youth group and in the Bible club on our high school campus. She wanted to go into full-time ministry after college. Her pastor's comments stunned her, and for the first time she began to question the only stable thing in her life. Where was God now?

God had earlier used her pastor to make up for the broken places in understanding the father image of God that was damaged by her dad's abuse. Now, her pastor's lack of understanding of how to handle her situation crushed her. Shauna didn't know how to address the issue with her pastor, so she didn't say anything at all. Her death was not her pastor's fault; it was a decision Shauna made. But we need to understand how some issues in the church can have devastating effects on young people.

Many young people's only lifeline is their church. In an earlier chapter I mentioned the verse "Fathers, do not exasperate your children; instead, bring them up in the training and instruction of the Lord" (Eph. 6:4). I believe God could be saying to us through this chapter, "Churches, do not exasperate your children; instead, bring them up in the training and instruction of the Lord."

Parent Power Point: Many teens feel their only lifeline is their church.

One way we can help kids is by giving them a role in the church, but we need to empower them to do that. In working with kids, I always share with them the verse "Don't let anyone look down on you because you are young, but set an example for the believers in speech, in life, in love, in faith and in purity" (1 Tim. 4:12). I challenge them not to wait until they're older to get serious about their relationship with God. If they don't like how the adults are living around them, I tell them to set an example for us. As they've tried to do that, the following issues are the ones that have been a hindrance to them. I've broken them down into the categories listed in 1 Tim. 4:12—speech, life, love, faith, and purity.

Speech

While I was growing up, I got the message that anger is bad. In church, an unspoken rule suggested that if you were anything but happy and content, that was bad. I knew I had to be a good girl in church and not disturb the people around me—which was a very good thing to learn, of course. But the message we got in church was that "children are to be seen but not heard."

I believe that is true of society as a whole, but the Church is working to turn this concept around. In the past 10 years we've seen a conscious push in Christian circles to acknowledge the problem and deal with it. We're making some great progress.

The generation of men and women who are now parenting teenagers grew up with the "children are to be seen but not heard" line of thinking, and many may still have a tendency to believe it. That's why it's important to acknowledge that anger is a natural emotion, and we don't have to be afraid of it. Again, since many of us as adults haven't dealt with our anger appropriately for most of our lives, we may be teaching our kids those same rules. If we can feel free to process our anger with our kids, they will see that they don't need to be afraid of their anger. Our example of dealing with anger can free them to see it as a natural emotion.

> Parent Power Point: **Since many of us as adults haven't dealt with our anger appropriately for most of our lives, we may be teaching our kids those same rules.**

In the Bible, the Book of James devotes a whole chapter to the subject of the tongue: "All kinds of animals, birds, reptiles, and creatures of the sea are being tamed and have been tamed by man, but no one can tame the tongue. It is a restless evil, full of deadly poison. With the tongue we praise our Lord and Father, and with it we curse men, who have been made in God's likeness. Out of the same mouth come praise and cursing. My brothers this should not be. Can both fresh water and salt water flow from the same spring?" (James 3:7-11).

Our young people are confused. Some of the inconsistencies at church are causing anger to well up in them. In church services they hear that they're to love their neighbor as themselves, but they don't know how to do that because of what they see lived out in the adults around them. It's as if we're saying, "Do as I say, not as I do." Teens can spot hypocrisy a mile off.

Another problem in church circles is a lack of acceptance of people who are different. In youth groups as well as everywhere else, we see cliques. It's difficult for kids to join a youth group because they are typically labeled as soon as they walk through the door by what they're wearing, their hairstyle, or other factors. How can we fault them, though?

At church we have "classes" of people differentiated by their education, economic status, marital status, race, family name, position in the church, and so on. Prejudice plagues churches, even between denominations. Churches of differing styles of worship and doctrine rarely come together.

In His Steps, a book by Charles Sheldon, has made a big splash among teens in the last several years with the "WWJD" slogan—"What Would Jesus Do?" I read the book in high school, and it strongly impacted my life. A few years ago when I saw kids wearing WWJD bracelets, I asked them if they knew what it meant and where the phrase came from. Very few kids had ever heard of the book. I encouraged each one to read it.

If you aren't familiar with the book, it features a church in a small town. One week a "tramp" went through the city looking for help. He had lost his job, his wife had died, and his daughter was sick. No one helped him. He stopped by a pastor's house, but the pastor was busy preparing his Sunday sermon and didn't have time to help the tramp.

The man showed up at the pastor's church on Sunday, and after hearing the sermon and songs about following Jesus in obedience, faith, love, and imitation, he knew he couldn't remain silent.

After the sermon, he walked to the front of the church. The people were shocked at his nerve, but he challenged them with the question of why they didn't do what they heard in the sermons and sang in the songs. Why did they ignore the needy in their midst when they professed love for all on Sunday mornings? The man then fell dead right before their eyes. The pastor was so moved by the intruder that he challenged his church for a year to ask the question "What would Jesus do?" and then do it. The book tells the story of what happened in the church and in individual lives.[1]

My purpose in sharing about *In His Steps* is to challenge us with "What Would Jesus Do" regarding the controversial issues we face.

If the tramp in the story of *In His Steps* had come to my church, would he have felt welcome? That's a question we all need to ask. If an obvious prostitute, homosexual, drunk, homeless person, or person of a different race entered my church, would he or she feel accepted? We must ask ourselves, "What would Jesus do?"

Jesus treated every person He met with dignity and respect. The woman who was caught in adultery in John 8:3-11 had been humiliated and shamed by the religious leaders. Yes, she had sinned, but what did Jesus do? When she entered His presence, she knew she had sinned, but Jesus treated her in such a way that her dignity was restored. He didn't shame her.

> Parent Power Point: **As we deal with the fallout from our teens' anger problems and confront them, we can think, "What would Jesus do?" and recall how Jesus approached other people, even hard-core sinners, with dignity.**

When I do something wrong and the person approaches me with Jesus' kind of attitude, I am empowered to make the changes needed. I look at the problem differently—with the courage to do something about it. If the person who confronts me shames me, it saps my strength and resolve, and it takes longer for me to deal with it. I question whether I am even worthy of a better situation.

Life

Many parents today grew up as part of the "me generation." We touted, "If it feels good do it," "flower power," "free love," doing things "my way," and so forth. We focused on ourselves, and many adults haven't moved past that.

Parent Power Point: We can't be so focused on our status, our careers, and our reputation that we leave our kids in the dust.

We're so focused on our status, our careers, and our reputations that our kids are being left in the dust. We don't have time to spend with them, or when we're with them our minds are on many other things. Just the cost of living can be a stress today, especially for single parents. Many of us are so stretched financially that we're living day by day and working extra hours just to make ends meet.

These societal pressures are taking a toll on our children and on us. There are more latchkey kids than ever before. The crime victimization rate for kids between 2 P.M. and 6 P.M. is the highest of any time of day because that's when so many students are home alone or hanging out on the streets or at neighborhood malls without parental supervision.[2] Most parents are distraught about these arrangements but can't do much about them. As a church and society we need to address this issue.

Our young people are crying out for our help. One teenager told me that he notices adults don't look teenagers in the eye. His words were penetrating, "People seem scared of me. They just look the other way when they walk by me. They don't even acknowledge that I'm alive. Instead of looking at me, they look at a pole or a store window. It's so obvious. I wish they would give me a chance to show them I'll smile back at them. It means so much when adults say 'hi' to me."

We need to reach out to the youth in our realm of influence. When you see kids, look at them and say "hi." Watch what their reaction is.

A lot of adults are afraid of kids today. I've worked with parents who are intimidated by their own children. I have found that teenagers are the same and have the same needs as when they were little—they just have bigger bodies and

What to Look for in Finding a Therapist or Psychologist

- Check with your insurance company about their procedure.

- Ask your school counselor, pastor, or others for names of people they would recommend.

- Fees vary greatly. Ask the therapist if a sliding scale (adjustment of lowering the fee to fit your income) can be used if your finances are tight.

- Over the phone, interview the ones that have been recommended to you. Ask about their training, degree(s), licensure. The advantage to having someone who is licensed is that he or she is under supervision and is accountable. Some nonlicensed counselors are good, but insurance typically won't cover them. Do your homework on this one.

- What percentage of their clients are your child's age? (If possible, you want to get someone who has a lot of experience in working with that age-group.)

- Ask about their experience in working with anger issues with kids.

- I recommend that you try to find a Christian counselor, but make sure he or she is a good one. If you needed brain surgery, wouldn't you want the best?

- When you and your child start meeting with the therapist, if either of you feels uncomfortable, find a different one. We open up better to certain types of therapists. If we find the right fit, incredible strides will be made. If it's the wrong fit, no one will get far in therapy.

- For more information, check out this Internet link: <www.grohol.com/therapst.htm.> "How to Choose a Therapist and Other Frequently Asked Questions Answered About Starting Your Psychotherapy." June 17, 1995. Last Revision: July 19, 1996. By John M. Grohol. This is a listing of other information to keep in mind while looking for a therapist.

express themselves differently now. If you're scared or intimidated by your kids, get help. Use the concepts found in this book and the volumes of information out there, but you need to get help from a qualified professional as soon as possible.

Love

Sex: this three-letter word causes parents to cringe as their children reach puberty. One thing you can be sure of: if your kids don't get the information from you, they'll get it somewhere else. Sex has long been the taboo subject that we've been reluctant to address at church, as if talking about it would cause our teens to become sex addicts. We need to be open to discuss the subject and make sure the youth directors at our churches are addressing it in the youth groups too.

In giving your teen proper information about sex, you don't have to sit the teen down and overwhelm him or her with all you know in one setting. Instead, look for teachable moments—for opportunities to bring up the subject.

For instance, when Cindy's daughter Kim rebelled against her upbringing and God and moved in with her boyfriend, Cindy learned that Kim was telling her 12-year-old sister, Ally, about some of her sexual experiences. Cindy realized that as reticent as she was, she needed to be proactive in talking about sex with Ally. One day when the time seemed right, Cindy asked Ally, "I know your sister has talked to you a bit about sex since she moved in with Matt. Has this raised any questions in your mind about anything dealing with sex?"

At first Ally was embarrassed to talk about it, so Cindy said, "Well, I just wanted to let you know you can ask me questions at any time. My mom never talked to me about sex, so I had a lot of confusion about it when I was your age."

Eventually, because the lines of communication were open and Cindy had expressed her availability and willingness to talk about this "adult" subject with her daughter, Ally came to her mother with questions about boys and sex and relationships. During these mother/daughter conversations, Cindy was able to address the subject of living with a boyfriend outside of marriage. She and Ally discussed what the Bible has to say about it so Ally could realize that even though her sister was practicing the behavior, it wasn't right.

> Parent Power Point: **Make sure your kids know you're available to address difficult issues and that no subject is "off limits."**

Teens today are bombarded with sexual messages everywhere they look. They may believe everyone else is involved in sexual relationships and that if they aren't there must be something wrong with them. When they choose to abstain from sex until marriage, they stand a good chance of being ridiculed and labeled "weird" by their peers. On the other hand, if they become promiscuous, they may be ridiculed for that and subjected to name calling by those same peers.

It's encouraging to see the abstinence programs that are making it into the public school curriculum. We need to explain to our kids that God has a reason for saying that sex outside of marriage is not His plan for our lives. God isn't a spoilsport. He created sex as a beautiful thing, but He also knows the potency of it and its ability to destroy lives when people fail to follow His guidelines for it.

If our kids fail to remain sexually pure throughout their teens, it is important that we as parents stand behind them and love them through it—just as we would through other difficult times in their lives, even though we don't approve or condone it. God can restore them, and we mustn't get in His way by withholding our unconditional love.

By the age of 18, 73 percent of young men and 56 percent of young women have had intercourse as compared to 55 percent of boys and 35 percent of girls in the early 1970s.[3] Today's teens bristle at the abstinence message when they see adults around them involved in adulterous affairs. They recognize and have angry reactions to the hypocrisy.

Another pitfall to be avoided is pornography. With the advent of the Internet, pornography is more readily available to kids than ever before, and there's an increasing awareness of the massive problem this has become in the Church. This vice is robbing marriages and families at a greater level than ever before. If anyone in your family is struggling with pornography, please get help immediately. The trail of destruction it leaves can be devastating. If kids know their parents are experimenting with pornography while telling them to avoid it, the result is distrust, disgust, and anger.

> Parent Power Point: **If kids know their parents are experimenting with pornography or affairs outside of marriage while telling their kids these behaviors are wrong, the result is distrust, disgust, and anger.**

You can help your teen minimize anger control issues by helping him or her learn to forgive. Forgiveness is an important spiritual truth with deep benefits.

The Church's approach to forgiveness is another area that bears discussion. In working with many abuse cases, I have seen a lot of hurt or confusion when Christians or church people have told those who have been abused to "forgive and forget."

Yes, the teen needs to be able to forgive and release their anger, but I have never known anyone who could forget abuse. Victims would love to forget the abuse, but forgiving is the crucial step, and true forgiveness will take time.

Forgiveness is somewhat like peeling an onion. You peel off one layer, and then another one gets exposed. Sometimes forgiveness—especially forgiveness for abuse—can take 10 or more years to process. It all begins with a willingness to forgive. In the forgiveness process, we forgive as much as we can each step of the way.

> Parent Power Point: **We can help our teens minimize their anger by teaching them to forgive others.**

Another aspect of teaching our children to forgive is that harboring unforgiveness generally hurts us more than it does the person who wronged us. If someone has hurt your teen, God will deal with that person. "Do not repay anyone evil for evil. Be careful to do what is right in the eyes of everybody. If it is possible, as far as it depends on you, live at peace with everyone. Do not take revenge, my friends, but leave room for God's wrath, for it is written: 'It is mine to avenge; I will repay,' says the Lord" (Rom. 12:17-19).

Too often teens spend a lot of their time and energy dwelling on what someone did to hurt them and all the while the offending person has moved on with life. Harboring bitterness toward someone actually affects us as if we were in a cage. It's as if we're trapped. When we keep dwelling on the wrong someone did to us, we can't move on with our lives. Our sons and daughters must understand that the key is in their hands. God can take care of the situation better than they could ever hope to. He wants to open the cage and set them free, but the teen must give Him that permission.

One characteristic that teens look for in adults is authenticity. If they see you hiding behind the facade that everything is OK when it's not, they learn to suppress their feelings, cutting off a part of themselves. If they cut off their negative emotions, they also cut off their ability to experience positive emotions to the fullest extent. For instance, love can be painful, but it can also be exhilarating. When teens cut themselves off from love and from life they often end up living in despair. If you've been hurt, let your children see how you deal with your pain so they will know how to face pain in their own lives. Talk to God about it. He wants to comfort you. And your kids will learn that He waits to comfort them when they are unhappy too.

> **Parent Power Point: Kids need to see how we deal with our pain so they will know how to face pain in their own lives.**

The picture of Deut. 33:12 comforts me: "Let the beloved of the LORD rest secure in him, for he shields him all day long, and the one the LORD loves rests between his shoulders." What a picture—snuggled up to God's chest between His arms! Jesus felt pain and hurt during His crucifixion that we could never fathom. He understands our pain, and He wants to help. One of the greatest gifts we can give our children is reliance on the Comforter in times of pain and disappointment.

Faith

Just as each individual must decide personally to accept Jesus Christ as Savior, so must each individual decide how far one wants to go in a relationship with Him. We can remain stagnant in the same faith we had 10 years ago, or we can grow to become all He has planned for us. The faith walk is one that our children will have to take for themselves. But they may very well base their faith in God on what they see in your life. You've probably heard the saying, "You may be the only Bible that some people ever read." What are your children reading in your life? What are your priorities? Who or what is your God? What do you think about the most or spend your time and money on? Do you "walk the talk," as they say? Do you live what you believe?

I'll never forget seeing my mom praying on her knees for all of us kids. My grandmother used to pray every day for all of her kids and grandkids. When she died, my aunt decided to take on that role for all of us.

Do your kids know you're praying for them? Are you praying for them? If you don't know how to pray, the only way you learn is through practice. God doesn't require any special words; He just wants to hear your heart. If you don't think you have time to pray, pray when you're in your car alone (keeping your eyes open, of course).

Studying the Bible is also vital. There are many ways to do that, and you can find the way that works best for you. You can also listen to the Bible on tape in the car. I've found that if I read my Bible every day, I have a better perspective on life.

Worry is a sign that you're not trusting God to do His part

in taking care of your kids. Pray for His protection every day and then leave them in His hands. (I know that's easier said than done.) You can't always shelter your children from the troubles of this life, because they must develop the skills to survive when they get out on their own.

Worry is a favorite pastime of parents—and it's no wonder! But if our kids see us worrying about them all the time, they'll wonder about the strength of our faith. We can be honest and tell them we're worried about them but then add that we're placing them in God's hands for Him to help them with whatever they face that day. It is so important to teach them to pray so when they are scared and don't know what to do, they'll turn to God.

> Parent Power Point: **We can be honest with our kids and tell them that we're worried about them—but then we can add that we're placing them in God's hands for whatever they face that day.**

Purity

In our world our kids have lost a lot of their childlike innocence. Young people are leery of adults who want to help them. They wonder if we're making them our "project." Even in the process of dealing with their anger, as we have discussed in this book, they wonder if we're doing it out of genuine love for them, because we're embarrassed by them, or simply because it's what's expected of us as parents. Sometimes we'll have mixed motives for what we do, but the most important thing is to be honest with them and live authentically before them. Again, that's why communication is so important.

If your relationship with your kids has been strained, reach out to them. Get to know them again. Learn the intricacies of their personalities. Tell them what you love about them. Look for glimmers of those innocent little children you once knew. They're still there. Look for the wonder of that child again. Pray for God to give you His kind of love for them. Celebrate who they are. Write them a card or note or send them an E-mail for no reason at all but just to tell them you love them and want a better relationship with them.

At first they'll be suspicious of the changes, but press on. They'll push away for only so long. In the midst of their struggle for independence, they'll know you're there for them. Give them wings to fly. When they go out and get scraped up by the world, knowing Mommy and Daddy love them no matter what will make it all better.

Kids have a zest for life, and we can learn so much from them if we just take the time to get to know them better. Looking at life from their perspective can be very refreshing. They go for the gusto in life and sometimes make mistakes that cost them dearly. But parents who diligently hang in there with their kids for the long haul will see their kids grab life and soar, while having the tools to face the changes in the wind. There is hope!

Action Steps

1. Are there issues that were covered in the chapter that apply to your teen's anger?
2. If yes, describe why you think this has become an issue.
3. What would be the best way to approach the topics with your teen?
4. List the key points you want to address with your teen, then plan for a time to meet and discuss the issues.
5. There's hope and healing only through Christ regarding these issues that can be prevalent in the church. Our hope is revealed through 2 Chron. 7:14—"If my people, who are called by my name, will humble themselves and pray and seek my face and turn from their wicked ways, then will I hear from heaven and will forgive their sin and will heal their land." If any of the issues listed in this chapter apply to your child, write a prayer as described in 2 Chron. 7:14.

11

Anger Harnessed

Ainsley epitomized an angry kid. Even though she became a Christian when she was young, her life was filled with extreme pain. Considering everything she has been through, it's surprising she is still alive. Ainsley believes the only reason she's alive right now is because of her mother's faith. If her mom, McKenzie, could get through to Ainsley, then almost any parent can get through to his or her child. Here is Ainsley's story of God's faithfulness in her own words:

As I was growing up, my family and I went to church every Sunday. Around the age of 12, I lost my aunt to cancer. She was only 22 and more like an older sister than an aunt. We were pulled into a nasty custody battle over my cousin. My stepfather was an alcoholic and had been using drugs for several years. My mother was in her final year of college, so she wasn't as available as she had been in the past. I knew she cared, but she was always busy.

Our church lost its pastor, and that was hard because he was the reason we started going to that church. The church went through a difficult time and was so focused on taking care of its own issues that our family problems fell through the cracks. When we needed them most, they were focusing on getting through their own struggles.

I was a very angry 13-year-old. I was angry with my father for drinking and not being home, at my mother for not being available, with my aunt for dying, and with my younger sibling for needing me. I was also angry at God. Why did He let this happen to my family? I felt I had nowhere to turn for comfort and support. So I went looking.

I could not turn my back on my family, so I turned my back on God. I wanted to hurt Him in the only way I thought I could—by turning to Satanism. It wasn't a very big leap for me, because I had been experimenting with witchcraft for over a year. I started reading up on witchcraft and Satanism. I'm an avid reader, but I also read to escape. Reading gave me an escape, and witchcraft gave me a feeling of control. I could feel God calling me back to Him, but I just turned my back on Him.

At the age of 15 I was raped by my boyfriend. After that, I shut myself off to the world. I became isolated by choice. I had friends and even boyfriends wanting to spend time with me, but I did not involve myself emotionally with those relationships. My mom was very concerned about me, but I wouldn't let her in. I knew she prayed for me.

Then we moved to California. My sister, who I was very close with, hated me for my family's move to California—she thought we moved because of my problems. She did not speak to me for about a year. She got into drugs to deal with our family's continual emotional roller-coaster way of life. My stepdad started drinking more. I tried drugs, but I didn't like them. I started drinking heavily instead.

Then we moved back to Colorado. When I was 17, my stepfather abandoned us. He went to work one day and never came home.

As my way of dealing with everything, I cut myself off from my family. So much was going on for me that I stopped hearing God calling me back to Him. I don't know why, but maybe it was because I didn't care about myself any longer, or anyone or anything else. I got pregnant but had an abortion because I didn't want to bring a child into my living circumstances. I fleetingly thought about God every once in a while, but I didn't dwell on those thoughts. I knew God was love, but I had nothing to love—not even myself. My sister used to compare me to the song by Simon and Garfunkel called "I Am a Rock," because I had no emotion or anything. I just didn't care.

My mom kept reaching out to me, but I told her to leave me alone.

When I was in my early 20s I met and married a Satanist. I knew that would really get back at God. Almost all of our friends were into Satanism, too, so I was surrounded by it. I drifted farther away from my family and friends because I didn't want them to know about my religious choice. I even stopped talking with my closest friend, Savannah, whom I had known since high school.

But no matter what I did, my mom wouldn't let me go.

Within two years I was separated and divorced. Then I reconnected with my friends and family. That was the best thing that could have happened to me. My closest friend, Savannah, was my biggest supporter, and my mom was my biggest "pusher"— someone who stands behind you and gives you a push (or in my case pushes) in the right direction. Her pushes were for me to go back to church and reconnect with God.

This was about the time when my mom met Shea, whose husband, Monty, was an interim pastor. Nita invited my mom to their church. Mom didn't have a car at the time, because she had loaned it to my younger brother, who worked most weekends. My new stepfather also worked on Sundays, so my mom volunteered me to drive her to church.

It was so hard to go back to church, because I didn't feel that I belonged there. How could God love me after everything I had done to Him? It was a very difficult church to go to because they looked down their noses at my mom and me. It was an affluent church, and we didn't fit in with that crowd. We drove an inexpensive car, while many of the members drove $50,000 cars. We didn't have the fancy clothes either. They were unwelcoming, uninterested in us, and uncompassionate. It was the most unfeeling church I had ever been in. I felt, *Who gave them the right to judge my family and me?* They did not know us nor did they want to know us. But despite this, or maybe because of it, God gave them a great spiritual leader in Monty. And perhaps that's why God placed me in that church.

I have had to overcome a lot to get where I am today. I would not be here if it were not for my mom. She never gave up. She kept on pushing and encouraging me. She still does today. Also I am thankful for Monty and Shea for their light and belief in the Lord. When Monty asked me to be a part of planting a new church as the youth director, I felt God smile and give me a little push. Through the church plant I am able to give something back to God for all the blessings He has shown me in my life.

Many times her mom didn't know if Ainsley would be dead or alive by the next week. But that never stopped the faithful prayers from a mom's heart as she kept storming the gates of heaven for her daughter, making sure God didn't forget about her little girl. I asked Ainsley if she would be willing to write a note to her mom thanking her for all she's done. Maybe someday you'll get a note like this from your child. "Dear Mom: Thank you for loving me even when I rejected you and your love. But I always knew that, no matter what, you would be there for me. Through those darkest years you always let me know you would never turn your back on me, and you never gave up on me. Thanks for being my mom. I love you, Ainsley."

Ainsley's pain has been healed, and her anger has subsided. She struggles with severe dyslexia, but she hasn't let that stop her. She earned a college degree, and her goal is to get her doctorate. Ainsley has touched my heart. My prayer is that Ainsley's story will provide hope for parents until their own story of healing has come to fruition.

Kids like Ainsley are why I do what I do. I have seen so many kids through the years with no hope for their lives. Some came from terrible home situations, but others came from homes with everything they could dream of. You have met a few of those kids in this book, and I'm proud to say they are my friends, and my life has been enriched by knowing them. I see God's face in their eyes.

I have shared some pretty brutal stories of pain and hurt in kids' lives. I pray that your situation is not as drastic. And although I have not seen many of these young people in a few years, I pray for them still.

God has given me a chance to share my heart with the kids I come in contact with each day. He has placed them in my life for a time and season, and when they leave at the end of their four years of high school, my prayer is that they will have felt the heart and love of God through me. I pray that the Lord would use me to fill in those places in their hearts that have been left vacant by abuse or neglect or just the harshness of being a teenager.

In the public school system I cannot share my faith freely unless the kids bring up the topic. But that's OK, because I can just love them anyway. The needs of kids from 1 to 18 are basically the same. They just need to know they are loved and accepted for who they are. I believe God has called me to be there when their parents aren't able to. Just to give them a smile, a high-five, or a pat on the back—I pray that they'll see God through me.

I've seen that even the most wounded kids can do incredible things! They need a cause, and they need adults in their lives who believe in them. I've seen the tough kids show great compassion for someone less fortunate. Kids give freely of what they have to help someone else. They need to know they matter. Let them dream.

Parent Power Point: Kids need a cause, and they need adults in their lives who believe in them.

Some kids at my school were touched to know there were 450 new orphans who lost both their parents as a result of the September 11, 2001, terrorist attacks in New York and Washington, D.C. They joined with other schools to collect over 1,400 teddy bears to send to those children. Kids care. We just need to give them a chance to show it. As adults we can empower them to do that. We can make a huge difference in their lives.

Maybe you're just beginning to deal with your teenager's anger issues. As I've been writing this book, I've been praying for every person who picks it up. I'll summarize my prayer for you in the acronym HOPE, which stands for

H—Healing

O—Opportunity

P—Perseverance

E—Enfolding

Healing

My prayer for you is for healing of all the broken places that have occurred in your heart that caused you to pick up a book like this. You may be thinking you have failed as a parent because of the situation you're in. You have not failed. If you had, you wouldn't be reading this book. You may just need some help in knowing the steps in healing your relationship with your child.

God knows your hurt, and He's saying to you, "Come to me, all you who are weary and burdened, and I will give you rest. Take my yoke upon you and learn from me, for I am gentle and humble in heart, and you will find rest for your souls. For my yoke is easy and my burden is light" (Matt. 11:28-30). You don't have to do anything before you come to God—just come as you are. He knows your needs. He knows your situation. As in the case of Ainsley, He just wants you to come to Him. He loves you and wants to help you. He wants to heal your child's anger problem.

Opportunity

The Chinese characters for crisis are made up of two symbols—one means danger, and the other means opportunity. The struggle with your child can be an opportunity. Even though it's not the type of opportunity you long for or would wish on anyone else, it's definitely an opportunity to grow. It's also an opportunity to get to know yourself and your child better. It's an opportunity to learn skills that will help you in any relationship you may encounter in the future.

You'll be able to face situations in a healthier way. You'll also have the opportunity to stop any cycle that may have been destructive in your family line. This is your opportunity to see God work on your behalf. It's a chance to break through fears and free your family to live more fully.

Opportunities take courage, which you have—it's obvious, because you've noticed and care about your teen's anger problem. My prayer is that God will use this opportunity to show you His love for you and your child in greater ways than ever before.

Perseverance

The process of dealing with your child's anger is going to take perseverance. I was a runner in school, but I was a sprinter. The long races wore me out; I didn't know how to pace myself.

The process you have enlisted in is not a sprint—it's a marathon. You'll need endurance to get through those tough times when you're tired and weary. But it will be worth it in the end. Once you get started on this journey, it may get worse before it gets better.

When you start implementing the changes, don't go back. For a while it may seem as if your kids hate you. Just remember that some day they'll thank you for it, because you'll save them a lot of pain. Your grandchildren will certainly benefit from your blood, sweat, and tears through this process.

My prayer for you is that you'll persevere through the tough times and know that, at the end of the race, you'll get the prize you have trained for—a child who will have the tools to resolve anger in a healthy way.

Enfolding

In the Special Olympics, at the end of every race, each runner is greeted by a hugger to congratulate him or her on finishing the race. I pray that you will feel that hug from God not only at the end of this process but also through the entire race. I pray that you'll have all the support you need to stay strong and complete the race.

I pray that you will feel the enfolding arms of your children as they run to you at the end of the race. They'll thank you for caring enough to hang in there with them through the tough times.

Twila Paris sings a song, "Runner," in which she depicts our running into Jesus' arms at the end of a journey. I hope you'll be encouraged by the picture of your running—tired and exhausted—into Jesus' arms at the end of your journey of trying to reach your angry teen. I can just hear God saying to you with a huge smile, "Well done!"

Action Steps

Is your child's anger problem resolved? Not yet? Take heart. You've come a long way. But remember, this process is a marathon, not a sprint. Review the previous chapters often for reminders.

1. What's the greatest accomplishment you've seen so far regarding your child's anger?
2. How has your child changed throughout this process?
3. How have you changed?
4. What's the next area you plan to work on?
5. In Phil. 3 the apostle Paul talks about pressing on toward the goal. Write a prayer asking God for His continued help and wisdom, for continued healing regarding your child's anger problem, and thank Him for His guidance throughout the process so far.

A Special Prayer on Behalf of Parents

Dear Father,

As a father, You understand the heart of every parent who has finished this book. Give these men and women the wisdom and discernment they'll need to press on in the journey that lies ahead as they continue to address their child's anger issues. In a way, this book isn't finished—it's only begun. Lord, I pray that You would encourage these parents. Please give them the strength to carry on during the difficult times when they don't see any progress. Father, uphold them and bring around them a support network of people who will be there for them during the tough times when they question themselves, experience fear, or lose hope. Lift them up and enfold them in Your arms as only You can do, Father.

I pray that You would bless these parents' efforts and cause their children to truly understand how much their parents love them. Perform a divine intervention in their children's lives to help them understand the severity of their problem and the consequences of their actions. As a result of the guidance and intervention from their parents, Father, turn these children away from a road of pain and rebellion.

Comfort the parents as they lay their heads on the pillow at night thinking and worrying about their children when sleep escapes them. When they feel like failures, help them realize that You hand-picked them to be the parents of their children out of all the parents in the world. They are the only parents through whom You'll be able to reach their child. Help them see that, with Your help, miracles can be accomplished in their children's lives. Even though it may seem impossible at times, with You all things are possible. Father, please give them the strength and courage they need to finish the race.

Father, I pray that You would bless these parents and pour back to them a hundredfold for all they've done and are doing to invest in their children's lives. Be with the rest of their family as these parents are trying to deal with a specific child's anger issues. Unify the family to work together well. Cause any other children in the family to be a part of the solution, not the problem.

Lord, give these parents a glimmer of hope and an anticipation of the future as You have promised in Jer. 29:11. Bring Bible verses or concepts from this book to their minds to help them each step of the way as they try to make changes, establish boundaries, or change the family dynamics that may or may not have contributed to the problem. When these parents are tired and low on energy at the end of the day, when it would be so easy to just go back to the old ways and give in, give them the strength to be consistent in following through with the parameters they have set for their children. When they fail, give them patience and grace with themselves.

Father, I pray that You would do an incredible work in each member of the family so that they can look back on this time in the future and see that You carried them through each step of the way. Open these parents' eyes to see Your fingerprints in these situations and how You are intervening and working mightily on their behalf. I pray that You would "restore the years the locusts have stolen" in these parents' and children's lives. Thank You, Father, that You care about what's going on in each of our lives and that You want to help bring restoration and healing where there has been destruction and turmoil. Father, we want You to be honored and glorified through this entire process so that we can be able to "comfort others with the comfort we have received." You are Jehovah Rapha—the God who heals. Lord, heal our children. We ask all these things in Jesus' name. Amen.

Notes

Chapter 1

1. "Quotes," compiled by Jen Noe, Internet site at
<www.geocities.com/rainforest/vines/6059/thoughts/quotes.html>.

Chapter 2

1. Barrett L. Mosbacker, *School Based Clinics: And Other Critical Issues in Public Education* (Westchester, Ill.: Crossway Books, 1987), 184.

2. Adam Cohen, "Criminals as Copycats," *Time,* May 31, 1999, 38.

3. Barry and Janae Weinhold, "The Cost of Failure," The Colorado Institute for Conflict Resolution and Creative Leadership, Internet site at
<www.weinholds.org/bullyfailure.htm>, 2001.

4. "Teens See Increase in Fighting at School," The Gallup Organization, Internet site at <www.gallup.com/poll/releases/pr001002b.asp>, 2001.

5. "Domestic Violence Is a Serious, Widespread Social Problem in America," Family Violence Prevention Fund, Internet site at <www.fvpf.org/newsdesk/facts/>, 2001.

6. Remuda Ranch, Internet site at
<www.remudaranch.com/communityed/communityed_pat.shtml>, 2001.

7. "Who Self Injures," Internet site at <www.palace.net/~llama/psych/who.html>, 2001.

8. Terry McCarthy, "Warning: Andy Williams Here. UnHappy Kid. Tired of Being Picked On. Ready to Blow. Want to Kill Some People. Can Anybody Hear Me? How Did Things Get So Bad?" *Time,* March 19, 2001, 28.

9. "Drinking, Driving, and Other Drugs," Mothers Against Drunk Drivers, Internet site at <www.madd.org/stats/Stat_youth.SHTML>, 2001.

10. Ibid.

Chapter 3

1. Robert Fulghum, *All I Really Need to Know I Learned in Kindergarten* (New York: Villard Books, 2001).

Chapter 4

1. Ted R. Miller; Deborah A. Fisher; Mark A. Cohen, "Costs of Juvenile Violence: Policy Implications," *Pediatrics,* January, 2001, 165.

Chapter 5

1. John Bradshaw, *Healing the Shame That Binds You* (Deerfield Beach, Fla.: Health Communications, 1988), vii.

2. Donald L. Nathanson, *Shame and Pride: Affect, Sex, and the Birth of Self* (New York: W. W. Norton and Company, 1992), 312.

3. Ibid., 313.

4. Ibid., 317.

5. Elizabeth Kubler-Ross, *On Death and Dying* (New York: Simon and Schuster, 1997).

6. William Pollack, with Todd Shuster, *Real Boys' Voices* (New York: Penguin Books, 2000), 313-14.

7. James Garbarino, Lost Boys: *Why Our Sons Turn Violent and How We Can Save Them* (New York: Anchor Books, 1999), 52.

8. Sheila Walsh, *Honestly* (Grand Rapids: Zondervan Publishing House, 1996), 70, 87, 79.

Chapter 6

1. Henry Cloud and John Townsend, *Boundaries: When to Say Yes, When to Say No to Take Control of Your Life* (Grand Rapids: Zondervan Publishing House, 1992), 28.

Chapter 7

1. Cloud and Townsend, *Boundaries,* 28.

2. Patsy Clairmont, *Mending Your Heart in a Broken World* (New York: Warner Books, 2001), 86.

3. Henry Cloud and John Townsend, *Boundaries for Kids: When to Say Yes, When to Say No to Help Your Children Gain Control of Their Lives* (Grand Rapids: Zondervan Publishing House, 1998), 19-21.

4. David Keirsey, *Please Understand Me II: Temperament, Character, Intelligence* (Del Mar: Calif., Prometheus Nemesis Book Company, 1998), 12.

5. Ibid.

6. Tim LaHaye, *Transforming Your Temperament* (New York: International Press, 1991), 16-27.

7. Gary Chapman and Ross Campbell, *The Five Love Languages of Children* (Chicago: Moody Press, 1997).

Chapter 8

1. J. B. Phillips, *Your God Is Too Small* (New York: Macmillan Publishing Company, 1978), 7-8.

2. Hannah Whitall Smith, *The Christian's Secret of a Happy Life* (Grand Rapids: Baker Book House, 1952), 15.

Chapter 9

1. Dee Brestin, *The Friendships of Women* (Colorado Springs: Chariot Victor Publishing, 1997).

2. Gerald Corey, *Theory and Practice of Counseling and Psycotherapy,* 5th ed. (New York: Brooks/Cole Publishing Company, 1996), 375.

3. Steve Karpman, "The Drama Triangle," Internet site at <www.ta-tutor.com/!dratri/xdrallp.htm>, 2001.

4. Steve Karpman, "The Drama Triangle," Internet site at <www.ta-tutor.com/zhandout.html>, 2001.

5. Karpman, "The Drama Triangle," Internet site at <www.ta-tutor.com/!dratri/xdrallp.htm>, 2001.

6. Steve Karpman, "The Drama Triangle," Internet site at <www.ta-tutor.com/!dratri/xdrsecp.htm>, 2001.

Chapter 10

1. Charles M. Sheldon, *In His Steps* (Grand Rapids: Spire Books, 2000).

2. Office of Juvenile Justice, "Comparing Victimization of Adults and Juveniles by Time of Day, 1991-1996," Internet site at <www.ojjdp.ncjrs.org/ojstatbb/html/qa117.html>, 2001.

3. Walt Mueller, *Understanding Today's Youth Culture* (Wheaton, Ill.: Tyndale House Publishers, 1999), 243-44.

Recommended Reading

Allender, Dan B. *The Wounded Heart.* Colorado Springs: NavPress, 1990.

Anderson, Neil T. *Victory over the Darkness.* Ventura, Calif.: Regal Books, 1990.

Carter, Les, and Frank Minirith. *The Anger Workbook.* Nashville: Thomas Nelson Publishers, 1993.

Chapman, Gary, and Ross Campbell. *The Five Love Languages of Children.* Chicago: Moody Press, 1997.

Clairmont, Patsy. *Mending Your Heart in a Broken World.* New York: Warner Books, 2001.

Cloud, Henry. *Changes That Heal.* Grand Rapids: Zondervan Publishing House, 1993.

Cloud, Henry, and John Townsend. *Boundaries: When to Say Yes, When to Say No to Take Control of Your Life.* Grand Rapids: Zondervan Publishing House, 1992.

———. *Boundaries with Kids: When to Say Yes, When to Say No to Help Your Children Gain Control of Their Lives.* Grand Rapids: Zondervan Publishing House, 1998.

Dobson, James C. *Parenting Isn't for Cowards: Dealing Confidently with the Frustrations of Child-Rearing.* Nashville: Word Books, 1987.

Garbarino, James. *Lost Boys: Why Our Sons Turn Violent and How We Can Save Them.* New York: Anchor Books, 1999.

Garbarino, James, and Claire Bedard. *Parents Under Seige: Why You Are the Solution, Not the Problem, in Your Child's Life.* New York: Free Press, 2001.

Kiersey, David. *Please Understand Me II: Temperament, Character, Intelligence.* Del Mar, Calif.: Prometheus Nemesis Book Company, 1998.

LaHaye, Tim. *Transforming Your Temperament.* New York: International Press, 1991.

Lerner, Harriet, *The Dance of Anger: A Woman's Guide to Changing the Patterns of Intimate Relationships.* New York: HarperCollins Publishers, 1997.

McDowell, Josh. *The Disconnected Generation: Saving Our Youth from Self Destruction.* Nashville: Word Publishing, 2000.

Mueller, Walt. *Understanding Today's Youth Culture.* Wheaton, Ill.: Tyndale House Publishers, 1999.

Nathanson, Donald L. *The Many Faces of Shame.* New York: Guilford Press, 1987.

———. *Shame and Pride: Affect, Sex, and the Birth of Self.* New York: W. W. Norton and Company, 1992.

Oliver, Gary J., and H. Norman Wright. *Pressure Points: Women Speak Out About Their Anger at Life's Demands.* Chicago: Moody Press, 1993.

Pipher, Mary. *Reviving Ophelia: Saving the Selves of Adolescent Girls.* New York: Ballantine Books, 1994.

Pollack, William. *Real Boys.* New York: Henry Holt and Company, 1998.

———. *Real Boys' Voices.* New York: Penguin Books, 2000.

Seamands, David A. *Healing for Damaged Emotions: Recovering from the Memories That Cause Our Pain.* Colorado Springs: Chariot Victor Publishing, 1991.

Sheldon, Charles. *In His Steps.* Grand Rapids: Spire Books, 1984.

Walsh, Sheila. *Honestly.* Grand Rapids: Zondervan Publishing House, 1996.

———. *Living Fearlessly.* Grand Rapids: Zondervan Publishing House, 2001.

Whitall-Smith, Hannah. *The Christian's Secret of a Happy Life.* Grand Rapids: Spire Books, 1952.

Wilson, Sandra. *Hurt People, Hurt People.* Nashville: Thomas Nelson Publishers, 1993.

Workshops, Parent Support Groups, and Related Internet Resources Regarding Anger

To find workshops or parent support groups in your area, check with your church, school counselor, local counseling centers, mental health organization, or local health department.

To find information in the Internet about anger, log on to a search engine and type the words "anger," "anger in children," "angry kids," "conflict resolution," conflict mediation," "support groups," and so on.

One note of caution is that you need to check carefully the credentials of the site's originator—the person, company, or organization that hosts the web site—to make sure they're qualified to be writing on the topic. Another thing to keep in mind is the philosophy behind their advice. Just because they have a web site doesn't mean they're experts in the field.